PRAISE FOR LONG WALK ON A DRY ROAD

"We are so grateful for our partnership with H2OpenDoors and Rotary International to bring the poorest people in Mexico what they need most...clean safe drinking water. *Long Walk on a Dry Road* describes Jon Kaufman's journey."

   - Vicente Fox, Former President of Mexico

"Kaufman's book taps into what is great when American passion meets the worldwide water need. Miracles happen, taps are opened, lives saved. Waves of Rotarians join his dream to give the gift of clean water, and ripples are created which change our world."

   - Barbara Metzler, author of *The Gift of Passionaries Changing Our World.*

"Jon Kaufman is a true Water Warrior: candid and focused, calling out problems with water charities that fail to empower communities in the long term, and showing a different way of sustained engagement with Rotary International. My singular hope is that Rotary can do for water scarcity and injustice today what it did for polio last century: eradicate these forms of bodily burdens and injustice. Jon Kaufman is your guide if you're down to earth and committed to making your efforts to make a difference, really make a difference."

    - Christiana Zenner, Ph.D., author of *Just Water* and Associate Professor of Theology, Science and Ethics at Fordham University/Lincoln Center

Water, enterprise, saving children's lives, this book is an experience of love at first sight. One of the most important books to read in 2018. My advice: dive into this book without delay! Woven with rich storytelling, you'll travel to the poorest areas of the world with Jon Kaufman's H2OpenDoors on a journey to bring self-reliance and dignity as much as access to safe-drinking water for every human on the planet. I found myself both laughing aloud, and teary-eyed ... and had only reached page 13. As Henri Matisse once said, "Creativity Takes Courage." *Long Walk On A Dry Road* is both creative and courageous!

    - Marlene Elizabeth, Author of *MoneyWings*™

Long Walk on a Dry Road is Jon Kaufman's invitation to you to move your feet, be bold and unapologetic, and take action to support whatever movement may be calling to you."

    - Linda F. Patten, President & CEO, Dare2Lead With Linda

"A must read, Jon has invited the world to share who he is and his ongoing journey to tackle the World's Water Crisis with a little technology and a whole lot of soul. The story is real, Jon's determination to do something about it is inspiring and his plan is working."

    - Jack E. Barker/Innovative Water Technologies, Inc.

LONG WALK ON A DRY ROAD

THE EDUCATION OF A WATER WARRIOR

Jon Kaufman

Founder, Director
H2OpenDoors
a project of Rotary clubs worldwide

RHG Media Productions
25495 Southwick Drive #103
Hayward, CA 94544

www.YourPurposeDrivenPractice.com

DEDICATION

Dedicated to the memories of Jaye Stroud, Barry Levine, Joseph Kaufman (my father), and also to Michelle Nirenstein, Ted Dibble, Jennifer Katz, Vicki Kaufman, Jim Zenner, Lea Dean, SC Moatti, Jack Barker and Team IWT, Kevin Sofen and the Darley team, Brad Harris, Alex Buck, Barry Jolette, Theresa Garland, Dawnet Beverly, President Vicente Fox, Liliane Sykes-Kwofie, Chief Edward "Ted" Makwaia, thousands of members of Rotary clubs, and to the Barefoot Engineers and Water Warriors throughout the world.

FOREWORD

Since my early days in the military to management in corporate and now as an entrepreneur who trains leaders and changemakers, I have a passion for the visionary individuals who want to change the world and are ready to take the practical steps to make that impact on a global level.

My work with clients—moving them through their seed of an idea for a movement into a force that is felt around the world—is likely why Rebecca Hall Gruyter introduced me to Jon Kaufman. She believed that Jon's book would resonate with me and my "troop." After a deep conversation with Jon, I knew she was right and that this book would be perfectly aligned with all that I believe about meaningful change.

Jon suggests we read this book from front to back, which was not difficult for me to do; I couldn't put it down. He has the vision for his H2OpenDoors project embedded in his psyche with every sense of who he is, and the personal story he tells is uniquely (and entertainingly) his. Clearly, he has made sure his vision is neither small nor static; rather, it's alive and growing as each new SunSpring system is installed in communities that otherwise would never experience clean water or a thriving water economy.

I related to his practical approach in bringing these communities to complete self-support—no quick handouts, but a deep involvement in each village in terms of their needs, their culture, and what is sustainable over the long term. Jon says, in his signature pull-no-punches style, "I don't want to protest about our systemic problems as much as I prefer to roll my sleeves up and do something. I've found hundreds of kindred spirits in the process. You'll not find us in a march. We're working in the trenches."

Through his straightforward delivery, open heart, and irrepressible humor, Jon took me on a journey like none I've ever had (or, I suspect, many other people have had!). The journey seamlessly blends the technology and business of water, how governments work (and do not work), tribal festivals, dignity and resilience in the midst of crushing poverty, voodoo, typhoons, exceptional leaders, and a man's personal story into one triumphant, heart-warming experience.

A special part of the story for me is how Jon's enthusiasm drew people to volunteer and travel with him to the water projects. They did indeed "roll up their sleeves" to "kickstart villages and schools who've been getting the short end of the stick for generations." I loved the fact that the adventurers not only worked alongside the villagers but also celebrated with them. They also got the rare opportunity to experience remote and exotic places that tourists seldom see and, in so doing, took part in discovering the next great location for clean water.

These (what I like to call) electric connections and allies supported H2OpenDoors' mission as Jon enthusiastically supported their own. Jon showed that he is no Lone Ranger trying to change the world by himself; he wholeheartedly embraces his "kindred spirits," recognizing his people and how grateful he is for their service. We see a beautiful display of how collaboration—not competition—can work.

It was the last chapter, *Ten Random Suggestions to Improve the World*, which really got me excited. Here, Jon give us the opportunity to pull out just one of these powerful suggestions and make it our own. What a gift this is to those of us who say, "I know I am meant to change the world, yet I don't know where to start or what to do." Here you have it.

I am so glad that I am able to bring my thoughts and feelings to you about this book. Jon Kaufman is truly a force of nature. His book tells a tale that the world needs to hear. People of the world have the right to clean water and the right to an economy that supports them. We as a nation have the opportunity to *pay it forward*, not only in the developing world but also right here in the United States. *Long Walk on a Dry Road* is Jon Kaufman's invitation to you to move your feet, be bold and unapologetic, and take action to support whatever movement may be calling to you.

~~ Linda F. Patten, Leadership Trainer for Women Entrepreneurs and Changemakers – President & CEO, Dare2Lead With Linda
Website: *www.dare2leadwithlinda.com*
email: *linda@dare2leadwithlinda.com*

CONTENTS

Introduction 13

Chapter 1 Labadie is on Haiti...*shhh!*
It starts with water / The education of a neophyte...........................17

Chapter 2 The Queen of Lamu
Our Magnificent 18... 29

Chapter 3 Hey kids, let's put on a show!
At Customs, it's customary / Fast forward to July 2018 /
Safari in the Mara 37

Chapter 4 Changing the Salsa Dance in Cuba
Why not try it in Nicaragua? / How do we choose where
to work?.. 55

Chapter 5 Voodoo on Good Friday
Rara groups The tip of Haiti 87

Chapter 6 Second Responders Matter
Finding answers / A pond of critters and super typhoon
Yolanda / Puerto Rico, FEMA and Math / When will we
get off the bottle? / Marketing Juggernauts 95

Chapter 7 The Fallacy of the Nonprofit
Plugging into a power pack of passion. 119

Chapter 8 Voluntourism as a Thing
The Good, the Bad and the Ugly / My favorite dopamine
surges / Gringo Epiphanies / Best day of my life / It
hasn't always been rosy 123

Chapter 9 Surrounded by Unsung Heroes
We don't have to look far to find our role models. 143

Chapter 10 Ten Random Suggestions to Change the World
Dialogue starters 147

INTRODUCTION

Best joke I've ever heard:

A guy spots a sign outside a house that reads "Talking Dog For Sale." Intrigued, he walks in.

"So what have you done with your life?" he asks the dog.

"I've led a very full life," says the dog. "I lived in the Alps rescuing avalanche victims. Then I served my country in Iraq. And now I spend my days reading to the residents of a retirement home."

The guy is flabbergasted. He asks the dog's owner, "Why on Earth would you want to get rid of an incredible dog like that?"

The owner says, "Because he's a liar! He never did any of that!"

Unbelievable, but true. I've had to crawl into my own head to try and articulate the incredible journey I've been on since the third act of my life began. This is my first book. Welcome. We all have an exclusive, personal play we are starring in, complete with an opening act, middle and closing. It seems that mine will be a bit more divided than others, as my life story is partitioned into neat, 17- year increments. Just worked out that way. Turning 52 (starting of Act 4) had set me off in new directions with unexpected obsession. Now, at the age of 63, with about five more years until the intermission, I figured I should jot it down. Maybe a few people will be entertained and even inspired to join my journey or start a new one of their own.

As you turn these pages, you will notice some bad words. They are not meant to offend. They slip out once in a while because that's also my voice. I use them for emphasis and hopefully to get a chuckle out of you. I've been told that certain publishers will redact these words for fear that book sales will suffer. So, I've tried to find a publishing house that accepts edgy, first-time writing. They will need to be large enough that I don't sink their fortunes, but small enough to give me a tryout.

I also want to warn you that my opinions are woven through every paragraph. Some of the conclusions I come to aren't necessarily evidence-based. You won't see an exhaustive appendix of footnotes and attributions. Just me talking. From my experience and through my lenses. If it rings true to you, that's good enough for me. If you want to call bullshit, then email me with your comments and review. I might respond, but I won't disagree. Unless you're like the schnook I met a couple years ago at the George Lucas School of Cinematic Arts at the University of Southern California.

In the main theater, I was asked to introduce the first short documentary of National Geographic's series on technology in the earth sciences. This particular episode was directed and narrated by Angela Bassett. I was asked to introduce the premiere of this series to an audience of film devotees and students by explaining the H2OpenDoors project. It was a great honor assigned by the series sponsor, AT&T.

With a day job running a Silicon Valley marketing company alongside two old and dear friends, I started the project as a part-time passion play. Jennifer Katz and Vicki Kaufman (my ex-wife and still dear friend) have afforded me far too much latitude to pursue this obsession. It requires that I travel through the world with a team of water and development experts to install purification technology in impoverished villages and schools with contaminated water. Health is improved and death is averted when you give people safe drinking water, or better yet, the equipment to process high-quality water from their own raw sources.

After my introduction, and after the screening, the lights came up and the crowd dispersed. I positioned myself at the foot of the stage to answer questions, with a small group of people waiting in a short line. The last two I will never forget, yet I have blocked their names out for reasons that will soon become evident.

They were USC professors. I did six months at USC following high school and quit to join a cult. Not really, but it was 1969 after all. I had no use for more school at the sage old age of 17. So my return to the campus some 43 years later raised my hackles a bit. These two guys, both wearing sweaters tied about their necks, holding files and papers close to their sides, approached with smiles and handshakes. The first one to speak says, "Mr. Kaufman, very interesting, your remarks at the beginning. You do realize that you are upsetting Nature's rhythms, don't you?" OK, I was hooked. "Please elaborate," I requested. Oh boy, was that a mistake.

"I've written several books on this subject," he sniffed. "When you and your friends impose on the natural laws, there are unintended consequences. In your case, you mean well, but trying to save lives by improving their water quality can have dire outcomes."

My response is an example of my attitude when faced with lunacy. "Was one of your books called *Mein Kampf* by any chance?"

This was not received well. But they deserved it. They live, day by day, in academia. The theoretical world. I live in the meantime. In the meantime, people are suffering, and I have the team assembled to help them help themselves. In the meantime, Nature will have to give me the opportunity. I am, we all are, part of Nature. Even those pretentious dopes.

Suffice it to say that AT&T never heard about my altercation. But whenever I meet a professor, my sphincter tightens just a little and I prepare for battle.

I'm not convinced that we are hard-wired to seek meaning and purpose. True North to me is that our default positions are more about the avoidance of pain and the pursuit of pleasure. Something can happen in our lives, however, some sort of awakening when we least expect it, changing our trajectory away from lives of quiet comfort or quiet desperation. We might have an experience of a random act of kindness, given or received. We might lose someone we really care about, and we begin to dissect why we loved them so much. We discover what they had, what they did that we were missing.

I've lost some essential friends and family this past year, as we all do. This book is my travelogue along a path of discovery about privilege and suffering, and that some of the poorest of the poor can feel more fulfilled and centered than we do. The people that I've met, and the new connections we make together, provide the best lessons for my journey.

It is a long walk on a dry road. But when you walk it with people you love, admire and laugh with... bring forward a mission you care about...well, it's *a great day at the beach.*

LABADIE IS ON HAITI...SHHH!

At around 2:30PM on July 25, 2009, pop superstar Michael Jackson died. The internet almost broke under the weight of the social media chatter, tributes and grief. Hundreds of thousands of spontaneous memorials and vigils took place in almost every country on Earth. I was clueless to all of this until weeks later.

My sister died that very same day, and I was with her at the time in Evergreen, Colorado. My son, Joey, was in the forest outside her mountain house, playing guitar and singing to the spirits to give Jaye another chance. I was cooking dinner and checked in on her only to see her take her very last breaths with a fixed stare into my eyes. This independent, beautiful woman was six years older than me. Always my protector and greatest cheerleader, Jaye was unconditional love. Cancer became her full-time job for four years. This is the nature of the disease. It takes you over, and you must pay attention.

One year before, when she was in between chemo treatments for the ovarian cancer that had spread throughout her body, we were on one of our annual play trips, this time a Royal Caribbean cruise. At the age of 59, her body just starting to show the signs of severe degradation, Jaye needed to prove to herself, to me and to her nephew that she still had a fight in her. She climbed the shipboard rock wall, attended the aerobics class, took me roller-blading on the top deck, and exhausted me.

One of those days, the ship pulled into the offshore anchor point for Labadie, the glamorous and beautiful vacation day spot owned by the cruise lines. This is a port stop on a small peninsula jutting out on the north end of Haiti, a small yet essential fact left out of the brochure. We offloaded from the ship onto an armada of smaller boats called tenders and made our way to the long piers for a day of food, music and beach.

Marimba bands greeted 3000 passengers, and staff directed us to the buffet of chicken, corn on the cob, potatoes, coconut and pineapple. We feasted at picnic tables and enjoyed the festive ambiance. We rolled our bellies over to the beach and kicked back in the sun for a couple of hours, taking in the surf and the view of the giant ocean liner we had come in on, floating just 500 feet away.

With the sun setting, we boarded our tenders once again, and set out for our return to the ship. My sister and I noticed that the cruise director on our boat was working overtime to keep our attention forward, towards the cruise ship. "Keep looking ahead to avoid sea sickness. Forward, forward," he would say with the pep of a game show host. We found this odd, so we did what my sister and I usually did...the opposite. We scuttled to the aft and looked at Labadie as we departed. We were mesmerized by what appeared to be 1000 Haitians descending out of the jungled mountains to the party site we enjoyed not five minutes before.

We watched this horde of people, full families with little babies in tow, riffing through the garbage, eating the remaining meat off the chicken wings, squeezing the last bit of mango juice from the plastic bottles, chewing any available kernels from the discarded corn cobs. Jaye and I started to cry, and we were without words for the 15 minutes until we docked at the floating platform of the sea entrance to the Liberty of the Seas. I had to say something. I made a vow to her. "Jaye, I will do something about this. I don't know how, but I promise I will." We hugged hard and long. We knew we were in the final stages of sharing life together, and we wept again.

From that day forward, I became obsessed with my promise to my sister. The entire trajectory of my life changed once I had spoken those words and got that response from her. The contrast of our afternoon together, in the lap of luxury, juxtaposed with the ravaging for food that we witnessed had me on full tilt. I could no longer look at buffets the same, or scenes of excess. I didn't particularly like myself at that moment, reflecting on years of relative privilege. "By accident of birth" became my mantra to understand how I was feeling. Not through any talent or effort on my part did I appear on the planet in 1954 to a life of middle-class comfort and love. I was never hungry, not for longer than an hour or so. I always lived under a good roof, hung around with others just like me in Los Angeles, California.

Sure, I had joined an intentional community in the late sixties and helped people with drug addictions. I even worked with many people to coach self-reliance and self-respect. I did this for *walking around money*, living a communal life from the ages of 17 to 34. But I never, ever had to dumpster dive and then return to a slum on the other side of a jungled mountain, defecate in a hole, and be in the total dark when the sun set.

Not unlike Survivor's Guilt, I became obsessed with being authentic and caring for the less fortunate. Before "the revelation," I cared only when it was convenient to do so. Or when I would receive a big pat on the back. Or when there was a tax advantage to giving a shit. I felt hollow, inner-directed and clueless of what my path was and where I was going. My only obligation was to raise my adopted baby boy, guide him through adolescence without him getting killed or killing someone else. I wasn't successful at that responsibility, but that's a long story to be told at another time and probably on a therapist's couch.

Baby boomers like Jaye and I remember the years of our roots. The late 60s and early 70s were transformative. These days, we talk a lot about "disruption." But back then, it wasn't about turning the taxi industry on its head with ride-sharing apps. It was more about discarding everything that came before us. We had been lied to about Vietnam, had our heroes assassinated right before our eyes, their replacements showing themselves as true character disorders. Trusting no one over forty was the safe way to navigate forward.

IT STARTS WITH WATER

Of course, I was many years older than the age limit for relevancy when I made the promise to Jaye. Out of the grinding grief I was feeling, I needed to disrupt something to get into the right groove. How could I do something about the suffering we had seen that day in Labadie/Haiti? What contribution could I make to offer some sort of difference that would honor the vow to Jaye? I surmised, without much of a leap, that water should be my focus. It all starts with water, doesn't it? Water is a scarce commodity. Future wars might very well be fought over water rights rather than oil. The poorest of the poor should be able to not only have access to safe water but should be able to earn a living from producing the liquid gold that all who walk the Earth need every single day.

In the United States, we are largely unaware of the fundamental importance of water. Since 1972, when Richard Nixon reluctantly signed the Clean Water Act, every American has a legal right to clean, safe drinking water piped right to their homes and businesses. This is quite remarkable. I would argue that this Act was the loudest declaration of human rights we've ever had since 1776 or 1863. In fact, no other country has adopted a mandate as sweeping and enforceable as the Clean Water Act. Our children have no idea how rare it is on Earth that you can go to any random garden hose in the United States and drink the water from it without fear of diarrhea or worse.

I began to pool the money I was making from my Silicon Valley marketing company to become a mini-philanthropist in the water space. I donated a large amount to a major international water charity, but in reading their brochures was troubled by the "gist of their gib."

I went to the board and shared my concern:

Jon to the Charity's Board: *Your marketing message is: "Last year we put in 1000 wells in Kenya. This year, we're going to put in 1000 wells in Ghana. So, send us money."*

The Board to Jon: *Yes, so what about it?*

Jon: *Well, what you should be saying is: "Last year we put in 1000 wells in Kenya, and this year we're going back to repair or replace the 60% that are inoperable."*

The Board: *We'll never be able to raise money that way.*

Jon: *So give me my money back.*

The Board: *We can't do that.*

Jon: *Why not?*

The Board: *We spent it on more wells.*

Most well experts will tell you that the more accurate figure is 40% of pumps and wells being inoperable at any one point in time. But during a Seattle visit to the headquarters of behemoth charity, World Vision, the director of water and sanitation worldwide told me their figure was actually 60%. Whatever that number, I knew then that I wanted to do things very differently. I would start my own 501(c)(3) qualified nonprofit. This is the IRS tax code section that allows donors to deduct from their income tax the value of qualified charitable contributions during the tax year. I would focus on water purification. I figured that the one thing we have on the planet in abundant supply is contaminated water sources. Why should we stick straws into the Earth as our go-to strategy? Most populations in rural areas have settled near lakes, rivers and ponds. Fresh water sources are everywhere and none of it ready-to-drink. Bacteria, cysts and viruses are present in almost all bodies of water. And yes, even well water can be polluted. Purification, Benjamin. Purification.

THE EDUCATION OF A NEOPHYTE

I spent a full year, in between doing my day job at the marketing firm, studying different technologies and approaches to water for the rural poor. Several years before, in 2000, the UN had published its Millennium Development Goals, or MDGs. This ambitious set of milestones aimed to cut in half extreme poverty rates, slow down the spread of HIV/Aids, and other goals by 2015. One of these metrics spoke to me the loudest: Cut in half the number of children, under the age of five, who die every day from waterborne disease. In 2000, that number was over 4000 per day. Think about that for a moment. Yesterday, 4000 kids died from diarrheal disorder. Today, 4000 more. Tomorrow, another 4000. By 2015, that number had reduced to about 2000. Great news, right? Right! The MDG goals put a sharp focus on the important stuff, and as a global community, we did something about the slippery slope of suffering.

Dig in a little deeper and you find all the MDG improvements were in urban areas. The rural poor have been left out of the improved infrastructure, healthcare investments and political rally. And those kids under five? Well, think of it this way: Imagine 11 jumbo jets, filled with children under the age of five. You see the headline "2000 Children Perish in 11 Fiery Airplane Crashes." The story continues, "The same thing happened yesterday, the day before, the day before that..." No big leap to watch the entire world coming together to stop the pointless airplane crashes. Our best minds would convene a technical task force to solve the issue and work tirelessly until the crashes stopped completely. Congress would unite, social media might forget about the latest celebrity scandal, and CNN and Fox News might talk about things that really matter.

Of course, we don't have daily crashes of jumbo jets. However, we do have thousands of people dying every single day from bad water. **The World Health Organization (WHO) estimates that half of all the hospital beds in the world are occupied by patients with waterborne disease.**

All this talk about diarrhea is probably ruining your dinner plans. Sorry about that. But why would an annoying bout with the Big D cause risk of death? I mean, we all occasionally get it, right? A little Imodium and we're good to go. The problem is what happens after a bout with *the D*. Your body is excreting electrolytes (salts and potassium) in a huge flush, dehydrating your entire system. If you don't rapidly replace the electrolytes and become rehydrated with safe water, your immune system takes a big knock down. Another bout, without rehydration, and your immune system is further compromised. In some cases, you are trying to rehydrate with the very same contaminated water that got you into this predicament in the first place.

If this is happening to your kid under five years old, or your grandfather, maybe over 70, that's even bigger trouble. With an immature or weakened immune system to start with, these Big D episodes cause a cascade of issues, leading to a shutdown of vital organs and potential death.

It's not always runny stools that cause havoc. Many times, illnesses are related to *not drinking enough water*. In some countries, bottled water is more expensive to buy than beverages like Coca-Cola. So, many drink sugary sodas, which are actually *dehydrating*. Stones develop when you don't drink enough water to flush out the crystallizing carbohydrates. These stones can form and grow in your kidneys, bile ducts, gall bladder. Last year, during a visit to the Helping Hands Hospital in Kathmandu, Nepal, I saw 12 people in the pre-operation prep room. I asked Gupta, the hospital administrator, what they were all in for. Eight of the twelve were scheduled for stone removal. All as a result of not drinking enough safe, drinking water every day.

By the way, humans should be drinking half their body weight in ounces in a day. Petite Ariana Grande should drink about 50 ounces a day. The Rock should pound 130 ounces. Of water—just water. You can't substitute iced tea or sodas. The quota needs to be met with water. Very few of us do this. And if you're exercising during the day, you need to drink even more to replace what you sweat and exhale out.

Ultimately, I didn't start a 501(c)(3) nonprofit. I spoke with my friend Gentry who works at GuideStar who, like Charity Navigator, keeps a check and tally on nonprofits. He told me that there are over 2 million nonprofits with 501(c)(3) status. 50,000 form every year, and 40,000 fold up. That's a growth rate of 10,000 new nonprofits every year. How many possible varied causes are there? Certainly, less than 10,000. Probably about 100 unique cause categories. Why so many new nonprofits then? I'll discuss the underbelly of the charitable world in another chapter.

Suffice it to say I joined Rotary instead. Established in 1905, today there are over 1.2 million members in more countries than the United Nations, with 35,000 clubs. It was the original social network, dedicated to service above self. I started the H2OpenDoors project within Rotary. How perfect, I said, hand wiping hand in that classic villain gesture. I've got a pool of over one million potential donors. I've got a universe of clubs in about any region I would want to work in. Those Rotarians can be my eyes and ears when I leave that country. I've got a built-in board for oversight. *Jon's the name, world domination is my game.* I shall use my power for good, not evil!

My year-long investigation of the appropriate technology to use for rural villages, schools and hospitals led me to Rocky Ford, Colorado. My friend, Mike Hom, used to work at GE Capital and told me that the only GE Imagineering award ever given out to a product that wasn't owned by GE was for the SunSpring. The manufacturer, Innovative Water Technologies, had started producing this game-changing system just three years previously, and a couple dozen were being installed in Haiti just weeks after the 2010 earthquake. IWT's solar-powered system was capable of cleaning up 5000 gallons of raw water every day. This was exactly what I needed to fulfill my promise and Jaye would smile down on me. As of this writing, we have 27 installations of the SunSpring water plants under our belt. We've put these into villages, schools and hospitals in 10 countries.

But rather than doing four or five each year, I *want to do* 500 *per year*. If that water charity can put in 1000 pumps and wells in Kenya in one year, with 40 to 60% breaking down for various reasons, I know we can do better than that.

Here is my execution plan for 2019: How about 500 water systems every year that don't break down at all? Each one wired up with a Cloud-monitoring, Internet of Things (IoT) smart box that tells the village technician and the factory in Colorado when there's a service interruption. Systems get back online within minutes to hours. I would be able to look at a big monitor in California of all the installations positioned on a giant world map, indicated by red, yellow and green lights. The green lights are "all systems go." The yellow lights tell me that a monthly service date is approaching or has been missed. Red lights mean what you might imagine–"*Oh shit.*" The system is down or the voltage or amp draw is off-kilter. All hands on-deck.

Perhaps the most important aspect of our innovations relates to encouraging establishment of enterprise at the village. The entire system can be on a mobile pay platform, allowing water customers to receive water distributions on a prepaid subscription basis. Financial innovations have become ubiquitous, even in places like Kenya and Uganda, for the past 10 years. M-Pesa, PayPal and dozens of other platforms allow payments, small and large, and recharge of accounts right on your mobile device. Because we want a controlled, sanitized, bottle-filling operation, we would establish a utility model, with a village bottling staff filling large clean bottles for wide distribution and sale, one-half of the current prices. These innovations are actually in development and deployment will start in 2019 in India.

Solving the global water crisis is going to need imagination and, unfortunately, will need a series of wake-up calls. Like the alarm bells going off in Cape Town, South Africa. Their issue, as is the case in a growing number of major cities, is more about water scarcity than quality. The taps are shut off for several hours through the day. Shut off. Day Zero is looming for Cape Town, when not even severe conservation measures will prevent taps from being shut off permanently. The UN's World Water Development Report warned that global demand for fresh water will exceed supply by 40% in 2030. Other cities like Cape Town are perilously close to their Day Zero. Included are the largest population centers on Earth: Mexico City, Jakarta, London, Sao Paulo and Beijing.

Water scarcity will soon affect most of us. Think of it this way. Picture the Earth as the size of a basketball. Drain all of the water to form a new all-liquid planet to now circle Earth. That would be the size of a ping pong ball. But since 97% of the water is in the oceans, and therefore undrinkable, the *fresh water would be the size of the head of a pin!*

And it's not like we get to manufacture water by some sort of chemical combination of hydrogen and oxygen. Wouldn't that be cool! No, the water that's available to us is the same water that a T. rex drank and then peed out, as much as 50 gallons of it!

In the book *The Big Thirst*, author Charles Fishman points out, "*Every glass of water you pour–whether it's coming from an Evian bottle, a filtered refrigerator spigot, or the kitchen tap–has a rich history.*" When you consider the amount of water that is simply flushed every minute in America alone, we need to get over our issues about "toilet to tap." Water can be cleaned–to perfect status.

Few governments have studied and modeled themselves on the Singapore experience. Twenty years ago, on a visit to this fascinating island nation, I learned about NEWater. The government's water utility was recycling and purifying toilet effluent, then bottling it with a colorful label and goofy little drop mascot. It has taken a full generation to accept this. Marketing, promotion, national pride as well. Singapore has positioned itself to be water independent through innovation and imagination. Giant bottling plants produce NEWater using membrane technology. The SunSprings are membrane systems with five miles of membrane strands. The NEWater plants are massive, with enough membranes to stretch to the moon and back. Cities should all be like Singapore and should have been working on this problem long ago. It will take a generation to become water independent, *so what are we waiting for?*

Many urban centers are so mired in bad piping and systems so old and close to complete failure that the only sensible thing to do is to start from scratch. Take Mumbai, India for instance. Back in 1970, a public/private partnership was formed called the City and Industrial Development Corporation, or CIDCO. The corporation had its germination some twenty years before that with regional planning work and government acquisitions of private lands. At the time, Mumbai, then called Bombay, was among the most dysfunctional large cities in the world. The water, in particular, was (and still is) filthy, toxic and in short supply for the burgeoning population. A brand-new metro center, to be named Navi Mumbai, was projected to become a master-planned community drawing one million people from old Mumbai with new industry and housing from the 70s through the 90s.

CIDCO planned and built all the railway stations, roads and public gathering places, while awarding commercial development to the best architects and builders in India. Currently in development is the Navi Mumbai International Airport. Navi Mumbai is a success story for about 1.5 million inhabitants today.

One of their more recent developments is Morbe Dam, now the town's primary source of water. India receives seasonal monsoon rain, and in most regions, infrastructure is rarely developed and available to capture huge quantities of rainwater to last throughout the dry seasons. The capacity of Morbe Dam is over 14 million acre-feet. I calculate that at over four trillion gallons of water. It takes vision and inspiration and decades of planning to create a sustainable system for large population centers.

CIDCO in India and the government of Singapore have demonstrated the power of foresight and imagination. But from insight to execution, multiple generations are required to take part in the baton race. Three or four decades are required to design, build infrastructure and promote a large city. It is, therefore, the responsibility of the citizenry to show outrage when leaders seem to waste time with ego-centric concerns or initiatives that don't move the ball on the important things. Entropy happens slowly but surely in our current urban centers, and we can't allow it in our country or in the countries of our brothers and sisters.

THE QUEEN OF LAMU

We had been planning our July 2018 expedition to Africa for almost a year. It was to be a three-act play. Umra Omar was our first beneficiary for this trip.

Umra is the founder and director of Safari Doctors and is the UN Person of the Year for 2017 and a CNN Hero. Young and plucky, Umra and her Ethiopian-born husband Zig personify the energy and ambition of modern Kenya these days. Only four years ago, she started to coordinate regular sailings of medical doctors and medicines to the people of the archipelago off the coast of Kenya. Based on the quaint island of Lamu, where only donkeys, camels and motor scooters are allowed as transportation, Safari Doctors sends several teams out on monthly sailings.

This NGO (non-governmental organization) owes its kickstart to motivational guru Tony Robbins. On one of their Golden Circle trips to little known but intriguing spots on the globe, Robbins gifted the fledgling upstart with a large cash infusion. Off and running, Safari Doctors serves the 20,000 indigenous Aweer and Bajuni residents of the archipelago and the Kenyan mainland near the Somalia border, providing the only medical services they will likely ever have access to.

At a dinner party in San Francisco, hosted by my old friend and supporter, Kate Beckwith, I met Umra. We began to discuss our mutual passion plays. I learned that she was not a medical doctor. I had an immediate connection on that level. While I design and install water purification plants around the world, I'm not an engineer. I thought, *"Two posers out to change the world."* I've found the best questions, most innovative solutions and strongest accomplishments are most often shepherded by visionaries. The technicians carry out that vision.

Umra is an inspiration to medical professionals and to a world-wide community of people looking for ways to provide medical care to the poorest on the planet. Over a fragrant roast and crispy potatoes with the Golden Gate Bridge in the background, I began to explain what we do at H2OpenDoors. While seemingly impressed, she was nonplussed about my assumptions that water quality is a major problem for the people she serves. After my usual line of questioning, I was astounded to hear her reaction to one dinner-inappropriate yet crucial question. I always inquire as to the number of children, under the age of five, that have chronic or occasional diarrhea. Umra answered dismissively, "Oh, of course there is diarrhea, but it's due to the children teething."

I shouldn't have looked so aghast at her answer. I've heard that bizarre, uninformed answer several times before. But not from someone I admired, and who headed up a world-renowned medical service. I began a long-winded explanation that:

a) The most likely reason for childhood diarrhea throughout the region was due to bacterial-infestation from their water source.
b) Most people believe if their water is clear, it must be safe.
c) While the assertion is that teething and excessive saliva are upsetting the young stomachs, it's actually the transition from mother's milk to water—contaminated water—that is causing diarrhea.

d) Immune systems are still developing in the very young and are compromised in the very old. These are the ages that are most afflicted with diarrheal disease.
e) Each episode knocks down the immune system's ability to stave off all other sorts of maladies.
f) Each episode dramatically dehydrates the body.
g) Death occurs to almost 2000 children every single day–every day–due to diarrheal disease.
h) The WHO says that one-half of all the hospital beds are filled with patients with waterborne disease.

I admit I'm not the most delightful dinner guest, but Umra was intrigued and open to this concept. I was pleased that I didn't hear defensiveness. But she wasn't particularly motivated to work on the issue either. Until I talked about enterprise and the potential to earn money for her NGO through the sale of purified water to her constituents and others in the surrounding regions.

A bright light went off in her eyes, and music played between us. People like us, anywhere in the world, are passionate about our missions. However, we all hate the one thing necessary to execute: fundraising. Most of us despise that we must ask for money.

"What if," I explained, "Safari Doctors could earn 30 to 50% of your budget requirements every single year through the distribution of safe drinking water?" We further pondered this cranial toggle switch and together supposed that pharmaceutical budgets, costs of testing and other medical services would flatten or decline as people were given a daily dose of two liters of purified water.

Over the next several months, Umra and I talked and texted on WhatsApp about installing a SunSpring ultrafiltration system on Lamu. At the Muslim village of Kipungani, she had arranged for a one-acre plot at the school property to be headquarters of this new business. Mai Water, "Water with Heart," was branded on hundreds of 10-liter family bottles. A borehole was created at just 45 feet, bringing up clear, but slightly contaminated water. We paid for a local solar team to come in, install a submersible solar pump and panels. Lab analysis showed that the only water quality issues were low levels of coliform (bacterial infestation) and a mineral taste. Our SunSpring installation would include a Granular Activated Charcoal (GAC) finishing stage once the water was purified through the membranes. The purified water would be bottled in one-gallon glass and 10-liter polycarbonate sanitized containers.

As we departed Nairobi's bustling airport en route to Lamu on a very small plane, I looked around at our participants for this latest expedition. Sitting next to me, Michelle Nirenstein is my person. We found each other a couple years ago when I spoke to her Rotary club in Woodside, California. Having been single for a while, and not able to find someone that found my life compatible with theirs, I had given up looking. Yet, we were soon dating and growing closer all the time. Michelle loves adventure and is the embodiment of Service Above Self. We travel well together, and now live with each other, along with our three dogs. A giant Alaskan Malamute, a tiny Mexican Chihuahua, and a mid-sized rescue mutt from Guatemala. Chaos ensues in a variety of sizes from all over the Western Hemisphere.

My eyes looked back a row at Jack Barker and my old friend, Liz Baun. I've known Liz for over 45 years, since she was eight. Jack is with me on almost every expedition. He is probably the most accomplished and experienced public drinking water expert in the U.S. More on him shortly, and throughout this book.

Mary Jo Bagger, who grew up with Liz. The most delightful human I've ever known, also since she was a pre-teen. Their friend Sheila, who lives around MJ and Liz in San Diego. This was her first exploit with us, and hopefully not her last. Alex Buck, an old friend of Michelle's, on his third or fourth expedition. Alex is an "all-in" guy–for friendship, for adventure, for commitment.

Dennis Bentley, a recently-retired waste water expert on his second trip with us. A Rotarian, Dennis is a great resource for our team. Ian Schmidt, Michelle's younger brother, joined our adventure. A soulful, engaged consultant to companies like Facebook, Ian specializes in helping get the most out of teams. Dan Smith, a member of my Rotary club, and his fetching girlfriend Susan. Dan is a Redwood City police officer and served in the Marines and in several embassies on security detail. Years before, he was stationed in Kenya and even played professional rugby for the Nairobi Harlequins. Susan has years of putting on big corporate meetings all over the world.

Ed and Rhonda Pierce, Ken Housely and Keith Marsh, all longtime Rotarians, providing an ever mature, yet fresh outlook. And our youngest member, Katarina, my dear friend Anna's granddaughter, took charge of the video camera every day. Keith was our master photographer. What he captured in his lens on the Mara, of the Milky Way, in all the interactions we had...pure art.

There were 18 of us, half members of Rotary, and half were other friends, from all walks of life. Each and every person added something unique and profound. I was very lucky. So fortunate that two "sisters from other misters" signed on. I've known both Anna Dibble and Wendy Williams for over four decades, and their husbands and ex-husbands have been some of my best buddies. Anna dove into her passion for folk dance on multiple occasions during this trip, and Wendy explored connections, as she does, with her passion back home as a US State Department Citizen Ambassador. I watched all these friends soak it in, getting filled up by it all.

On the morning of July 4th, fitting as the American Independence Day, our armada of boats loaded our entire team and set out for a 25-minute trip up the island coast from our swanky digs to the impoverished but charming village of Kipungani. We were welcomed by dozens of school children from the secular school, and from the madrassa, bedecked in their head coverings. Musicians played up from the beach as we were brought into a glorious dance circle. No words needed to be exchanged in those first magical minutes. We had all come together to celebrate and rejoice. By the afternoon, we had completed the installation of the SunSpring and the launch of the Mai Water enterprise.

Most of our group also worked with the children to install a large garden at the school, planting vegetables and herbs. Anna took the helm by providing leadership and innovative suggestions about crop rotation, efficient use of water and soil strategies. The sprouting crops will help feed the school, and the experience of creating it with the children will provide us emotional nourishment for years.

As we all gathered for a celebration dinner at a surprisingly fine restaurant in Lamu's old town, we toasted to independence and to sustainable solutions. We bonded, over the seas and over cultural differences, in spite of politics that might divide us. We are all brothers, sisters and friends. And we can't wait to return next year.

At that dinner, we bestowed a special lapel pin and certificate on one of my best friends and a man who is a soulful entrepreneur, Jack Barker. As the inventor of the SunSpring and President of Innovative Water Technologies, Jack has been our source for the water systems we've been exclusively using for six years. I had submitted a request to Rotary International to award Jack with the coveted Paul Harris Fellowship. Luminaries like Jonas Salk, Dwight Eisenhower and John Kennedy have received this honor over the decades, even though they weren't Rotarians.

It is a high honor, but the great honor I felt was the privilege of making the presentation. With nine Rotarians forming a half-circle behind Jack, I almost got through my introduction without being an emotional wreck. Jack makes the H2OpenDoors project possible with a system that is perfect for these kinds of applications.

More than a supplier, Jack and his company are consistent in their support and participation of our vision. His invention is quite amazing, and he holds a patent on solar-powered water purification systems which is even more astounding. It is fully automatic, capable of producing purified water even through the night. The current versions have no consumables, making the cost of operation around zero. The required monthly maintenance takes only 90 minutes and can be accomplished by anyone after a two-hour training session. SunSprings form the core of bottling operations and public water dispensaries in more than 400 locations around the world. The fact that they operate every day, off the grid, is the reason we need them now, more than ever.

The Lamu installation is especially important because it is exactly what we have set out to do from the very beginning. The name H2OpenDoors is a mashup of two concepts. First, *water technology*, intended with the scientific moniker. Secondly, the technology ought to be robust enough to make it possible for villages and schools to *start an enterprise*, providing funds to support opportunity for its residents and students. Opening the doors, giving opportunity to succeed. This is how generational cycles of extreme poverty can be interrupted. Those who disagree, write me an email. I would be genuinely curious about your reasoning.

The same communities that are water stressed also have other social services crumbling for lack of funds. **So, the mission of H2OpenDoors is as much about *enterprise and self-reliance* as it is about access to safe drinking water.** The average working poor in developing countries spend about 1/3 of their daily income on water. As outrageous as this is, the profits go to multi-national companies in most cases. Coca-Cola, Pepsi, Dannon and Nestlé control 80% of the bottled water industry, selling under hundreds of labels. We propose that the rural poor be cut in on that action and possess the equipment to produce their own quality water for themselves and for resale.

In order for a system to be contributed and installed, we require all the parties involved to sign on to a Memo of Understanding, adhering to several basic rules. One absolute requirement is that no individuals may profit off these sales. All revenue must go to the water council for disbursement on social service needs, like nutritional programs, agricultural development, classroom expansions, improved sanitation, even college scholarships. Violate any section of the MOU, and H2OpenDoors will remove the system. The local Rotary club or NGO partner monitors all aspects of our agreement.

In the case of Lamu, Safari Doctors will use all of the net revenue from their water sales for the expansion of services to thousands of people they serve with medical care. The provisioning of water in sanitized, refillable bottles does one other fundamental service. It promotes dignity. I have a photo on my desk of an old woman in Uganda, stooped in a river, sucking water through a Life Straw. This gadget, and many others like them intended for the weekend camper, is shameful to use in wide distribution, in my opinion. I use the Grandmother Test when I review solutions to everyday problems. I ask, "Would you want your grandmother to use this device every day?" The poor need to be treated with dignity. They deserve to have the same human rights that you and I do. They don't deserve to squat in a river or dip a jerry can into a lake or defecate in a hole they dig. Let's stop supporting unsustainable solutions that don't promote dignity or daily life improvement.

After three busy days on Lamu, it was time to continue our expedition. A short puddle jumper back to Nairobi, and then off to Tanzania the next morning.

HEY KIDS, LET'S PUT ON A SHOW!

Flushed with a "Mission Accomplished" sense of swagger, our 18-member Guardians of the Galaxy boarded a small plane from Nairobi and headed off to Mwanza, a city on the southern banks of the massive Lake Victoria in Tanzania. From there, we would be driven to Shinyanga Town three hours away. Surreal rock formations color the landscape in this region. Boulders the size of Volkswagens balance on top of others the size of semi-trucks, teetering on others larger than a three-story building. Some provided secure headquarters for these chiefdoms in centuries past. Many are now home to hyena families.

Shy Town, as the locals call it, is the geographic center of the Sukuma people, the largest ethnic group in Tanzania. Numbering almost nine million, over 80% of Sukuma still live in rural areas and are represented in 20 or more tribal chiefdoms. The Busiya chiefdom calls this region home and Chief Edward "Ted" Makwaia is its enigmatic leader.

Responsible for over 52 villages and 700,000 residents, Chief Makwaia inherited his role from his father and grandfather. Much loved and revered by the flock, the Makwaia legacy was sidelined from 1963 to just around 10 years ago. Tanzanian society, after a few decades, recognized that the chieftaincy had value after all, with attention to cultural affairs and input on local government.

Chief Ted, as he likes to be referred to, was an executive in charge of IT for the Central Bank of Tanzania for many years and has since taken on his role as Chief of the Busiyas and keeper of its rituals and beliefs. His soft-spoken nature and mastery of several languages belie a strength that over 750,000 of the Busiya respect deeply. In 2017, we had brought 16 participants on an expedition to Nhobola village to install a SunSpring system and bottling plant, followed by a safari in the Serengeti at the end of the Great Migration. This was H2OpenDoor's first work in Africa. I didn't want to work on the continent at all. You almost always have to drill wells here. I just didn't want to do that. Give me a lake, a river or any fresh water source, no matter the pollution levels. We'll purify the water and be on our merry way.

My reluctance was based on an estimate I heard from World Vision's head water dude, that 60% of the wells and pumps in the world, at any given time, are inoperable. Yep, you heard that right. Sticking straws into the Earth is more complex and less sustainable than sipping your cherry Icee. Who knew?

But then I heard about Chief Ted and the Busiyas and one particular village called Nhobola. Friends of friends ran a medical team out of Weill Cornell University, performing annual clinics at the village. In this driest region of Africa, 800 families had access to their own oasis of sorts. Known far and wide as Talaga Springs, a hand-dug well was created to capture the underground river of clear water. Palm trees sprouted around the springs, and this idyllic area became known as Nhobola's sacred spot.

Never mind that the water, as it gathered in the well, became contaminated with bacteria and was home to large families of frogs. It was liquid in the middle of a dustbowl. An old Chinese-made diesel pump was sending this water to a 25,000-liter elevated tank about 1/4 mile away. The tank, filled every day at least twice, drained to 13 different pipes throughout the village. A simple flow meter was at each valve, showing cumulative liter counts.

This was astounding to me. The people of Nhobola were not only paying for their water, but it was on the honor system. The village water council had never been "short" of payments, their old coffee can always holding the right number of TZ Shillings as compared to the total meter readings.

I called Jack Barker at Innovative Water Technologies. "You're not going to believe this, Jack," I said with almost breathless excitement. "I think I found my African village!"

Jack: *But you said you'll never work in Africa. You hate drilling.*

Me: *This is different. They have a spring! The water is contaminated. But they pay for the water!*

Jack: *How about in the dry season?*

Me: *They still have the water! Did I mention they pay for it?*

Jack: *When do you want to go?*

Me: *Let's go in October 2017.*

Jack: *But it's July. That's only three months.*

Me: *I know, let's get busy.*

This is my relationship with Jack. We've travelled to Haiti, to the Philippines only a couple weeks after the super-typhoon killed 7000, Mexico, Guatemala, Nepal, Nicaragua, Puerto Rico soon after Maria pounded the region in 2017... we've done 27 installations together over the past six years. That's at least 27 cigar celebrations with a Scotch and laughter after.

We've also been in some hairy situations during our travels. I've had a gun put in my face, we've been stopped on a rural road in Haiti by drunken rah-rah groups, been ripped off of our tools while we slept on a hospital floor in the Philippines. More than once, Jack has found me doubled over a toilet or hole puking my guts out along with the Cipro tablet he offered me. I've counseled him through his nasty divorce, he's listened to my various insecurities, we've shared our experiences raising sons with special needs.

Jack has had his own harrowing tales even before he met me. Following the 2010 earthquake that brought Haiti to its already broken knees, Jack lived there for five months. Installing 30 SunSprings at schools and community centers, providing the only viable safe drinking water among the chaos, he almost succumbed from dysentery. Jack scraped together contributions from the Clinton Foundation and others. Today, there are over 60 systems on this island nation, the poorest country in the Western Hemisphere, with a total capacity to provide 600,000 people with their daily drinking water.

Tanzania was yet another adventure to go on and an opportunity to bring over a dozen friends to join us. The Jack and Jon Show must look funny from the other side. I remember a teenaged Mickey Rooney in some black and white movie saying, "Hey kids, let's put on a show!" I want to put in SunSprings all over the world and bring my friends and families on our adventures. Jack's company has built a remarkable system that creates safe drinking water out of polluted rivers, ponds and lakes. His patented system is in over 400 locations, and there has never been a system failure in the 10 years since he drew the outlines of it at his desk in a former jeans factory in Rocky Ford, Colorado. Each SunSpring has the capacity to provide two liters of daily drinking water for 10,000 people without fuel, electricity or chemicals. This fully-automatic piece of technology has made it possible for me to fulfill my promise to my sister, over and over again. But it ain't easy, and I've made a ton of mistakes along the way.

AT CUSTOMS, IT'S CUSTOMARY

The first African Expedition was in the works. Our crate for Tanzania arrived in Kilimanjaro Airport Customs at the end of September. Chief Makwaia had insisted we send it there because of friends at the airport. Extraction would be a piece of cake. This is usually a load of bullshit, by the way. The issue with this extraction was a common one. I don't want to pay the Value-Added Tax (VAT). Customs is requiring me to pay it. In this case it is $3600USD.

VAT is a tax intended for commercial goods and is payable at the point of importation. What seems quite normal to brokers and customs officials all over the globe, makes steam pulse from my ears.

Jon: *I won't pay a tax for the privilege of contributing a gift to the people of (fill in the blank country).*

Broker: *No problem. We'll hold it in storage until you decide to pay it.*

Jon: *How much is storage?*

Broker: *About $500 per day.*

Jon: *Wait. What?*

Tanzania was no different. I paid the VAT and reported to Chief Makwaia how outrageous this was. As a former executive at the Central Bank, he was aghast when I told him. "Chief, the Tanzanian government doesn't want people like us to offer any help to the people of your country," I said. "They just charged me $3600 on top of other fees to tell me never to do this again."

And so it goes, over and over again. The Chief has a letter on the President's desk protesting this. Still waiting for a general waiver on VAT for Tanzania. I'll never get it.

We run into this in Mexico as well. Vicente Fox, the former President, is a great supporter and friend of Rotary in general, and the H2OpenDoors project in particular. We've installed five systems throughout the country and each time get hit with a

VAT (called IVA in Spanish) of 16% of the commercial value. That's about $3400 per unit. Here are some items on the approved list that brokers can charge 0% VAT:

1. Chocolates
2. Bottled water
3. Musical instruments
4. Sports equipment
5. Caviar
6. Gold jewelry

Random much? Because *"Water purification equipment given as a gift to the rural poor of your freaking country"* isn't listed, we pay $3400 each time. President Fox is flummoxed by this, as even he is not able to resolve the issue in Mexico.

In many countries, customs is a way to mine gold. Guatemala was the most colorful example in recent years. In the Fall of 2015, the President, Vice President and Treasury Secretary were arrested by the Guatemalan Supreme Court. They had been informed that every Tuesday afternoon, a helicopter would land at the Presidential Residence of Otto Perez Molina with pallets of cash... from customs. The corruption charges forced Molina to step down, and a special election for the Presidency was initiated.

Two people were put forth. One was Sandra Torres, a popular first lady from 2008-2012 when her then-husband was President. The other candidate was Jimmy Morales. With no political experience, but national recognition as the star of a weekly comedy sketch show with his brother Sammy for 14 years, Morales offered a fresh start and no corruption.

Jimmy won by a landslide. This is before the United States had contemplated a real estate man-turned-reality show star as a presidential prospect. The people spoke. You can't make this stuff up!

I digress! Back to Tanzania, I paid the ransom, and our crate was on its way to Nhobola village. We finalized our plans for 16 adventurers, my girlfriend Michelle and Jack to fly with me to Africa for 10 days of Service, Soul and Safari in October 2017. We installed a state-of-the-art bottling plant. We seeded the business with 1000 brand new, gleaming five-gallon water bottles. These family-sized bottles get sanitized prior to filling in a special room with a chlorination sanitizer apparatus we shipped. Bottles get delivered to the huts, empties picked up, and the water issue has just been disrupted and solved for 800 families. They see this as innovative and life-changing. We see it as simply the application of a distribution method long used in America. Even to this day, many of us get water deliveries in the same five-gallon hard, polycarbonate plastic bottles.

I prefer to control the cleanliness of the water containers in this way. You'll see 99% of international water projects with hand pumps and wells. For small communities of up to 200, this is an appropriate technology. And you'll observe lines of women with buckets, funky jerry cans and any container they can find. This works out alright, since the water they are pumping isn't purified. But a different system needs to be employed when you are taking groundwater, removing all the pathogens, and purifying it to the quality we enjoy out of most of our taps in the USA. So we provide family-sized bottles similar to what you see on top of water coolers. These are reusable and contain several days of drinking water for a small family. Going one step further, we like to see a small group of water warriors employed to deliver and exchange the empties, collecting a very small fee for the service. The money raised, by the way, can be significant each month. Many of the social services of the village or the school can be completely paid for out of revenue of these water enterprises.

The business at Nhobola was off and running, and a proud report from the Chief was emailed to me in California after the first month that 500 families were subscribing to the water service. The water bottles were being branded with the Talaga Springs name, and I felt like a new proud papa as I read the Chief Ted's report.

FAST FORWARD TO JULY OF 2018

Our new expedition arrives at the Tanzanian village of Nhobola following a magnificent installation in Lamu, Kenya, a celebration feast with the entire town and excitement from Safari Doctors, our new partners in water, education and peace. We make a beeline to the SunSpring to find *it is shut off.* I look at the meter reading, and it says only 7000 liters have been dispensed since installation. All the air leaves my lungs.

The village executive explains to me that the Tanzanian government had shut down their operation until the Tanzania Bureau of Standards (TEBS) gives approval to sell water.

Jon: So *don't sell the water right now. Give it away for free. The women and the children need safe water to drink.*

Village: *We tried to explain that, but TEBS won't even allow that.*

Jon: *So they will allow you to continue to distribute contaminated well water, but not purified water?*

Village: *That is correct. And we feel that if we push too hard on their logic, they will never approve our operation.*

Here is a piece of advice for anyone reading about this journey who wants to make a difference in the world. Prepare for a cartoon existence. There are times when everyone around you becomes characters in a *South Park* episode. Cartman, Kenny, the whole gang.

The Chief, not wanting us to run away I guess, never informed me of any of this, even though we've been having regular communications. One of the most pervasive afflictions on the planet is FeLoFa, Fear of Loss of Face. In America, we are rude and obnoxious and we like it that way. We want to hear when things are turning to shit. In fact, we have an entire media industry that makes sure we hear about it. In other parts of the world, "yes" means maybe, and "maybe" means not in this lifetime.

Our 2018 mission to Tanzania this time had four tasks:

1. Review the water project at Nhobola.
2. Attend the SabaSaba Festival put on by the Busiya Chiefdom for the eighth straight year.
3. Survey a second village for a 2019 water system.
4. Install a RACHEL educational system in the Nhobola Secondary school.

Task 1: The first task was reviewed and I decided I would leave suicide or murder for another day. It took eight months for TEBS to finally get around to give the seal of approval for the purified water's quality. But they are still waiting for final project approval to start the enterprise.

Task 2: The SabaSaba festival was 90,000 villagers, a couple white folks from the Peace Corps, and eighteen H2OpenDoors Adventurers. Tribal dancing, singers, python snake charmers and hyena wranglers delighted the throngs, all with an infectious back-beat of drums and ritual. Our H2OpenDoors team was treated as Guests of Honor. All were presented with gifts from the Chief and the Elders before the festivities began. The men, one by one, were presented with a shell necklace by a Sukuma chief. The women received a hand-carved cooking spoon. We were quite moved and honored.

Then the festivities began in earnest for several hours. The Chief and his council slowly worked their way through the crowds, flanked by security in robes, carrying spears. Forming a V behind them, all dressed in our purple H2OpenDoors shirts, we followed like colorful ducklings while the crowds parted, allowing us through. We were escorted to front row viewings, next to the leadership to view the cattle dancers, and then we all moved to the snake charmers, and then to the drumming circle, and so on. From the air, it must have been quite a sight. And all of it choreographed by the ever-watchful eye of the Chief's grandson, Nico. With but a raise of an eyebrow, Nico calmed large groups and restored decorum when needed. This 28-year-old man, with a new baby at home, is truly impressive.

The Chief asked me to climb up to the platform with him and address the crowd before we left late in the afternoon. He handed me the microphone. I spoke in English, and Nico translated. I don't know if anything was lost in translation, but it was a surreal two minutes. Looking out on a sea of black faces dressed in tribal attire, some smeared with yellow ceremonial paint and holding spears and traditional fighting sticks, called dlala 'nduku, I felt strangely accepted and appreciated. I get nervous when I'm in front of my small Toastmasters meeting each Thursday in San Mateo. This was different. I spoke about potential, and about traditions and about the respect for culture. I spoke on behalf of our 18 team members who learned so much today and that we are in your debt. The crowd was quiet as Nico translated to Swahili. It was remarkable. The drums, the bells, the python dancing, the whistles...all was quiet as 90,000 humans on the Earth paused, reflected and shared a moment.

I sat on the van back to town with Joseph Makwaia, the Chief's brother. Quiet and dignified, Joseph rarely smiles or shows any animation at all. Since I've known him, I see this as a challenge I welcome. I love to make him laugh. But I had a serious question for him. "Did anyone at the festival really know who the heck we are?" I asked. Joseph looked at me with a quizzical glance. He began, "All 90,000 knew exactly who you all were. They know you are friends of the Busiyas and of the Chief. They know about the water program at Talaga Springs. They know that they want this desperately at their own villages." We sat in silence to let that soak into my exhausted brain. I thought about how 90,000 people, without internet, learn and communicate through person to person storytelling. I drifted off to a deep nap, dreaming of beehives.

Task 3: The next day, we broke off into two teams. Four people were on the Water team, and everyone else was on the RACHEL Team. The water survey at the second village proved to be quite promising. When you look into the eyes of the elders at a village who have, as their daily charge, the provisioning of water as the most precious commodity, you are making a commitment. It is a solemn promise just by your showing up. Nhobola has to get things back on track. For themselves. For the new village. For the very lives of the people we are saying we are going to help. They show you where they live. Their children greet you. This is profound.

Task 4: The RACHEL team, meanwhile, was in a full court press. Remote Area Community Hotspot for Education and Learning is a wonderful, USA-made solution for rural poor who lack internet and a decent educational curriculum for children in Grades 3 through 12. World Possible is the NGO behind RACHEL, and my first experience with it was at a colegio in Guatemala where we had installed a SunSpring a couple of years before.

A flash-drive server about the size of a small pizza box contains all of Wikipedia, the full Khan Academy curriculum, the Great Books and thousands of tutorial videos. With one terabyte of capacity, it can also be loaded with local, cultural content, and is available in a number of languages. For Tanzania, we used the one in Swahili and English.

RACHEL provides it's own internet hotspot, pushing the content out to 100 *computers, laptops, tablets and smartphones.* The Khan Academy methodology converts teachers into learning facilitators, turning on the room with clusters of research and excitement about discovery. The teachers in the training session were invigorated and engaged. You could see it, you could feel it.

The RACHEL training session was in a computer lab with our 14 enthusiasts, six teachers from the school and Jackline John, World Possible's representative in Dar es Salaam. It turned out that Jackline is originally from Shinyanga and had particular insight into the underlying core issues the teachers have been dealing with. This included a scourge of child marriages, as young as age 14.

Classroom education for these rural communities is hard enough. In many cases, you've got 50 to 100 kids in one room. Little or no light. A couple ragged textbooks to pass around. If you're lucky, you have chalk. Add to these burdens the fact that babies are having babies. As a teacher there, if you want to have a conference with a struggling young student's parent, you probably should be talking to her husband who legally bought her the semester before. Chilling. I like to think that things can be different now that RACHEL has come to town. The kids of Nhobola have a chance to gain confidence as they grow older. Who knows?

We like to say about SunSpring and RACHEL that some of the most vexing challenges we have can be solved with a little technology–and a whole lot of soul. Our 14 expeditioners on the RACHEL team did some soul injections that day. As for the water program in Nhobola, we are assured that the Tanzania Bureau of Standards will soon give their final stamp of approval. In the meantime, four other Sukuma chiefs were with Chief Ted at the big SabaSaba festival.

"Other chiefs of Sukuma tribes joined us today in solidarity," Chief Ted told me. "We were all asked by the President of Tanzania, just last year, to provide two things for our villages–fix the water issues and create enterprise. Well, for eight months we've been waiting for the Tanzanian government to approve what we've established at one of these villages and then get out of the way. All five chiefs are requesting a meeting in Dar es Salaam with the President." I would love to be a fly on that wall. What happens at Talaga Springs is being watched by the leaders of nine million Sukumas. They are growing restless.

Chief Ted's cousin, raised with him more as a sister, is Liliane SykesKwofie. Founder of ASMK Foundation, Liliane focuses on the needs of the Busiyas with specific emphasis on the children of Shinyanga Town and Nhobola village. With about a dozen projects running simultaneously for IT and vocational training, clothing and nutrition, ASMK and the all-volunteer staff even offer opportunities to girls afflicted with albinism.

Liliane and her husband Sam, a retired dentist, live part time in Ottowa, Canada, in Ghana and in Tanzania. This couple is a powerhouse, bringing together resources in big ways. Whether it's the creation of a preschool, bringing in medical programs from the USA, or coordinating the work of H2OpenDoors to provide water and educational technologies for the villages, Liliane and Sam are solid partners. Together they started ASMK, named after her grandmother, Anna Schubert, in 2008, raising over $250,000 to renovate the hospital of her birth in Shinyanga. Kolandoto Hospital, built back in the days when Tanganyika was a colony of Germany before the First World War, had fallen in serious disrepair. The birth hospital of Chief Ted, Liliane and most of the clan that makes up the hierarchy of the Busiyas has a profound emotional bond with the facility and the community surrounding it.

Liliane retired from the United Nations High Commission for Refugees (UNHCR) to raise her children in Ghana, birthplace of their father. Today in Tanzania, she provides wraparound services for this community of her youth. In so doing, a visitor gets the sense of optimism and progress in these villages. Agriculture is the lifeblood of the Sukuma Busiyas in this region, made challenging by the arid climate. But with the development programs and innovations being brought in by Chief Ted and Liliane, the best days for the Busiyas are ahead of them.

SAFARI IN THE MARA

It was time for us to move on for safari in Kenya. When we arrived in the Mara on a dirt field in a plane that fit just our 18-member crew, we were ready to relax into the Maasai warmth and hospitality. Perhaps the best-known of all African tribes, the Maasai, or Masai, is a unique and popular tribe due to their long-preserved culture. Despite education, civilization and Western cultural influences, the Maasai people have clung to their traditional way of life, making them a symbol of Kenyan culture. Their distinctive dress style, graceful presence and strategic territory along the game parks of Kenya and Tanzania have made them one of East Africa's most internationally famous tourist attractions.

The Maasai people reside in both Kenya and Tanzania, living along the Rift Valley and border of the two countries. They are a smaller tribe, accounting for less than one percent of Kenya's population, with a similar number living in Tanzania. Maasais speak Maa, a Nilotic ethnic language from their origin in the Nile region of North Africa.

The warrior is of great importance as a source of pride in the Maasai culture. To be a Maasai is to be born into one of the world's last great warrior tribes. From boyhood to adulthood, young Maasai boys begin to learn the responsibilities of being a man and a warrior. Their sacred role is to protect their animals, and all wildlife, from human and animal predators, to build kraals or Maasai homes and to provide security to their families.

Through ceremonial rituals, including circumcision, Maasai boys are guided and mentored by their fathers and other elders to become a warrior. Although they still live their carefree lives as boys, they must also learn all of the cultural practices, customary laws and responsibilities they will require as elders.

An elaborate ceremony–Eunoto–is usually performed to "graduate" the young man to the status of a warrior. Only then can he now settle down and start a family, acquire cattle and become a responsible elder. In his late years, the middle-aged warrior will be elevated to a senior and more responsible position during the Olng'eshere ceremony.

The Maasai women do most of the work in their villages and run a burgeoning handicrafts business. The delicate beading they accomplish is some of the most intricate in the world. Michelle and a couple of her friends have a particular interest in this culture. Serving on the board of Friends of Maasai, Michelle bought a 10-acre parcel in the Mara. This will become the site of a 100,000 square foot Maasai Conservation and Learning Center. The first of its kind to honor the deep cultural roots, the center will also become an international destination on its own for anyone interested in wildlife conservation and the Earth sciences. Before anything can be built, of course, they need water. H2OpenDoors brought the team to the site to survey and begin to plan for a deep-water borehole and a SunSpring installation in 2019.

With a stick as a giant pencil in the dirt, Maasai leaders Harris and Amos drew out their vision for us. Each member of our party has since pledged funds and will become founding sponsors of the Center.

The Mara, during the Great Migration each year, is an experience like none other. Owing to the massive size of the herds, the wildebeest's movement stands out from other migratory movements as they move to the Mara from the Serengeti. How the animals know where to find food and water remains largely a mystery, but researchers have developed some hypotheses about the behavior. Most evidence indicates that weather patterns and the cycle of the rainy and dry seasons have the greatest influence on the wildlife movement. Because rainfall and weather are somewhat unpredictable, there is no way to calculate concretely where the animals will be at any point in the year, nor how long they will remain in one area. A reliable appraisal of their movement is only possible by studying historical data of previous migrations years. The majestic 1800-mile clockwise route of more than two million animals is a most fascinating aspect of the natural world.

Safari guides in the Mara love to show the wildebeest arrival and crossing of the Mara River that occurs around late July to August with parts of September and again on their return south, around the last two weeks of October through early November. While the sight of masses of animals thundering across the open plains is spectacular, the Mara River crossing will take you through a range of emotions: awe, anticipation, heartache, inspiration, excitement and much more. The crossing is the subject of many documentary films, from the BBC to the National Geographic, but even superb film-making cannot give you the experience of being on-site. Throngs of wildebeest gather on ledges above the river, and you can sense their urgency and hesitation. The energy in the air is palpable.

I love to see the zebras with the wildebeest. While traveling in far fewer numbers, the zebras seems to look and act like umpires, guiding the herds in the best directions. At least a million wilde-beest, 250,000 zebras, and 350,000 Thompson's gazelles (Tommies) participate in the parade. The zebras pioneer the way, delicately snipping the tops off the grass. The wildebeest are never far behind, mowing down the stalks to about an inch off the ground, and the nervous little Tommies prance along at the back, pulling the remaining tidbits from the ground with their elongated snouts. The feeding habits of these species complement each other as they cycle through the plains. Eating different parts of the grass ensures they are not in competition for the same food and can all herd together. The zebras can then keep watch through the long tendrils of grass for prowling predators, while the wildebeest keep their nose to the wind, and the Tommies constantly twitch their ears detecting the slightest slither through the waving blades of grass.

All along the way, predators lie in wait. The herds are a windfall of opportunity, which they wait for all year and use to train their young to hunt. The herd's epic travel means they are always in unfamiliar lands, always in another predator's hunting ground, never quite knowing which tree or termite mound may cloak long fangs and sharp claws. Leopards, lions and crocodiles attack the herds at will, and the hyenas and cheetahs pick off the small and weak.

An estimated 750,000 animals die during the migration each year, but many are actually killed by the herd itself, trampled in frantic, unorganized motion. Therefore, the herd brings both safety and peril. It is insulating and erratic, preserving life, and often a cause of death. However, both in life and death, the herds give back to the plains that nourish them.

The herds do not just graze the grass; they actually also help catalyze its growth. Animals leave a fertilizing trail of saliva, dung, blood and bones across the plains. The herds leave an estimated 3,620 tons of dung per day, which the dung beetles diligently roll and bury with their eggs. This ensures that arrival of the next rains will spur healthy regrowth. It is a great circle of life from the rains that grow the grass to the grazers that feed on it, providing food for the predators and fertilizer for the earth. You witness this in person, as it is happening, and you are changed forever. You place the human species into this scenario and lament that we take more from the Earth than we give. We could learn much from the herds.

CHANGING THE SALSA DANCE IN CUBA

Here's a great Jeopardy challenge: What island nation is known for its shape and is sometimes referred to as "El Cocodrilo"? What is Cuba, Alex.

Largest of all the islands in the Caribbean, Cuba's population is 11.5 million. Surprisingly, there are over 4000 smaller islands and cays. The average Cuban receives $17 a month. A Cuban has to work 57 hours to buy a 400-gram packet of powdered milk; in Costa Rica it takes only 1.7 hours. The system is failing.

Most Cubans are leading a hand-to-mouth existence, doing whatever it takes to feed their families–legal or otherwise. Hard-wired into the Cuban profile, however, are a couple of astonishing, contrasting facts. First, they have a 98.5% literacy rate. Second, they have 70,000 qualified doctors. My God, the entire continent of Africa has just 50,000.

I've always thought that Cuba is doing a sort of political Salsa dance...one step forward, two steps back. A frustrating place to try and do business, made even more impossible by the Trump administration's indifference, Cuba confounds even the most experienced.

Bob Schwartz, the head of Global Health Partners, is one of our many collaborators. For a couple dozen years, GHP has moved millions of dollars-worth of vital pharmaceuticals and medical equipment to the Health Ministries of both Cuba and Nicaragua. He regularly clinks cocktail glasses with the Cuban elite. Bob's organization is dedicated to navigating through the complex bureaucracies of the US Commerce and State Departments and the Parliamentary brick walls of Cuba.

So it seemed like a slam-dunk to be able to help the people of this tormented nation with the rebuilding of their hospital water systems following the hurricanes of 2017.

The Health Ministry: *Please, Bob, ask H2OpenDoors if they will help us at 11 hospitals. Here is a license.*

Bob: *Jon, will H2OpenDoors raise $300,000 over the next couple years to rebuild the water quality at these hospitals?*

Jon: *Sure, Bob. Let's do it. We need to start with a water lab analysis of their current water quality so we can configure the equipment at the factory.*

Bob: *OK, Jon, no problem.*

That was over a year ago. No water analysis. Radio silence on the matter. Cuba's ministries work in silo-like isolation from each other. The left hand doesn't know what the right hand is doing. That's why there is a specific list of visas issued. You can't combine your work with the Health Ministry with a People to People tour, as an example that has us stuck currently at the time of this writing. On our October 2018 trip to Havana, I wasn't even allowed to visit the Havana hospital to do a site survey because it wouldn't have complied with our People to People visa.

We work in regions throughout the world that throw festivals for our expeditions to show us their gratitude that we give a fuck. They recognize that we're not the usual NGO. We contribute and volunteer our time and funds from our own pockets. We travel to all parts of the world to do the service work and then to immerse ourselves in their culture for a week or two.

Whether it is Nepal or Nicaragua, Haiti or Tanzania, we get the feeling we are lighter than air, buoyed by our hosts' spirits and thankfulness. We can't help but think in all of our endeavors that "by accident of birth" we have plenty and they have so little. We operate on these expeditions in almost a dreamlike bliss from the moment we start planning the logistics to the moment Jack Barker and I light our celebration cigars after a successful installation.

But Cuba is different for me. I feel like I am working in a swimming pool of chocolate pudding, with lead weights on my ankles. Perhaps this is the nature of a capitalist do-gooder working in an established communist structure. It saps my enthusiasm and energy. The dark bureaucracy in Cuba, combined with their OppositeLand counterparts in Miami make it just about impossible. Most communist countries have the same challenge to us capitalists trying to work there. The bureaucracy is really about sectors of emphasis. The Health Ministry has a singular focus and has no input or interaction with the Office of Tourism or the Ministry of Foreign Investment and Economic Cooperation.

The new President, Miguel Diaz-Canel, has six–yes, six–vice presidents. All are members of the Communist Party and some serve on the all-powerful Political Bureau. A highly-experienced and respected team, we hope they will carry on the reforms started by Raul Castro. But tethered to a system with myopic missions and hampered by a 60-yearold US blockade, the Cuban government isn't any easier to navigate without the Castro Brothers. No one took a refreshing, deep breath when Raul stepped down. It's going to take a heretic, someone in either the United States or in Cuba who can convince the entrenched cold warriors that cooperation, mutual respect and trust are the best ways forward. No such leader is on the horizon.

However, they do have a brand new constitution. And as you read through it, you feel that Cuba just might very well come out of this darkness. It will take another generation, but the outline for freedoms and fairness are now, finally, in place.

On our 2018 trip to Cuba, twenty of us experienced a unique People to People tour curated by the Center for Cuban Studies. With a focus on the vibrant culture of today's Havana, I got completely new insights that I didn't appreciate when I brought 40 there in 2016. This time I learned how Santeria, the complex blending of beliefs and ritual practiced in many Caribbean regions, has roots in Nigeria and the Yoruba people. Cuba and Haiti are the best know practitioners but have differing emphasis. In Cuba, Santeria, or Regla de Ocha, is painting on a canvas of Catholicism. Layers of voodoo, home-based spiritual counseling and a hierarchy of priests and priestesses are evident once you begin to pay attention to the symbolism in all the art, dance and music.

Cuba is a rich patchwork that amazes and captures your imagination, with irony and contrast on display everywhere you look. From the ragged, yet grand architecture, to the rhythms of the classic jazz combos, to the Afro-Cuban thumping beat, much of what you will experience is unique to this island nation.

Proponents of the embargo are loudest in Miami. Many are children of those brutalized or jailed by the Castro regime. They argue that without a transition to a classic democracy, the United States will look weak. Only the Cuban elite stand to gain from open trade, they insist. Opponents of "el bloqueo" or blockade maintain that it is a Cold War relic and has failed to meet its goals. They say that the sanctions prevent change and democracy in Cuba by crippling opportunities for a rising middle class. The mortal enemies of Today's Cuba are some of Yesterday's Cubans living just 90 miles away from Havana.

Vendettas are hard to overcome, but they must be set aside. Revenge seems to be the only explanation for keeping up a 60-year-old blockade of goods and services. I don't buy the arguments that the only people who will benefit from the lifting of the embargo are the Cuban elites. Marco Rubio and his buddies have that wrong. I would wager that not one of them has stepped foot on Cuban soil, spent two weeks with the real people, walked through the Havana streets, or gone to the eco farms and tobacco growing regions. They don't really know anything about today's Cuba, nor are they interested in knowing. Gandhi's quote applies here: "*An eye for an eye only leaves the whole world blind.*"

President Trump has started the *retreat from anything-Obama* by implementing a new Cuba travel and financial restriction regime, effective November 2017. US visitors to Cuba must once again travel with an organization rather than on their own. "Individual people-to-people nonacademic educational travel will no longer be authorized," according to the US Department of Treasury.

Oh, what a difference one year makes. When I brought 40 Americans with me in 2016, Obama billboards dotted the Cuban landscape. They love our 44th. I was floored that to a person the optimism of what the future might bring was reflecting off of every smile I encountered. Back then, we held a cocktail party with 80 Havana citizens. Our combined 120-count group in the main ballroom of the Hotel Nacional was a microcosm of all the potential. Sure, we had capital-P party watchers from the Politburo. But we were there to listen. We broke into four conversation groups: Water & Infrastructure, Small Business, Education, and The Arts. The room was on fire...in a good way. To say the vibe was electric is too trite. I left Cuba a couple days later feeling on top of the world with friends who have struggled but felt very close to breaking the chains of the US blockade. A reform-minded Raul Castro was privatizing many of the business sectors, and President Obama was slowly but surely encouraging the opening up of our relations.

One of the Havana residents who came to the event out of sheer curiosity had a profound take on the evening. Omar Perez, a poet and observer of Cuban life for all of his 61 years, commented to one of our hosts, Felix, "This is the first time in my entire life that I've witnessed Americans and Cubans in such quantity having intelligent conversation." It wasn't lost on me that Omar is the son of Che Guevara and was an infant when the embargo began to choke the island.

A couple days before the Havana cocktail party, our crew spent a day at Corcovado, a village in Granma province. Fidel Castro was born in the area on the central southern coast. The town's 1400 residents have no access to purified water and carefully use their rationed supplies of bottled water. Piling into a 1950's-era bus without ventilation and seats for only half of us, we barreled down rocky dirt roads, dodging oxen-pulled carts with unfiltered water tanks. The project had been in coordination with a small NGO working in this region to put a SunSpring system in Corcovado, after connecting the aquifer from an adjoining small village called Nuevo Mundo. They were never able to secure the approvals to bring the water to Corcovado, and so we had to scuttle plans for an installation until we could get a provincial permit. We have waited two years, and we'll wait another two. We proceeded with the expedition anyway and did our site surveys in hope that we might be allowed to help these residents some day.

Upon arrival at the village, we were greeted by the "mayor." Jose Madero showed us to a shady portico off the main house, specially constructed for our arrival. Slaughtered goats and a huge pig were on manually-turned spits over smoking charcoal. The picnic tables were set, adorned with Cuban flags. An older guitarist was playing Cuban standards.

Each one of our participants had brought a suitcase filled with donation items we were going to present to the community leaders, along with the provincial representative of the Communist party. I pulled Jose aside and explained that everyone put a lot of thought into what they wanted to bring to this community. Pointing to

Brad Harris, I explained that as a baseball coach in his hometown when his kids were of Little League age, he has brought baseball gloves, balls and bats. Jose's eyes lit up. Some of our group went off to look at the water systems we were planning to modify, and Brad, Gary Albitz and others organized a spontaneous baseball game on a large dirt field.

"We chose up sides," Brad recalls. "We thought we would just have young kids to play with, but soon dozens of people showed up. Handing out the equipment it became immediately apparent that many of these guys were the second coming of Roberto Clemente." Brad led the teams in yoga stretches, much to the delight and laughter of the players. Brad pitched curve balls and Gary was catcher. The game became USA vs. Cuba. Midway through the 3rd inning, most of the little town appeared, complete with a cheer-leading squad. The center fielder was the team leader. At bat, he hit a towering fly ball that missed an ox by inches. It was a classic Grand Slam. The game ended with a tie, and our water group had returned to enjoy the feast that was being prepared.

The Cubans all lined up to return the equipment to Brad. "No, these are for you," Brad told them, continuing to hand 100 new baseballs to the kids. Later, at our formal gift presentation ceremony, Jose thanked Brad. "Todos somos hermanos en los deportes...Cubanos y Americanos." Jose had pronounced that "We are all brothers in sports...Cubans and Americans."

Turns out that the Corcovado baseball team was considered the best community team in Cuba for many years. It was Ernest Hemingway who helped with organizing community teams in the 1950s. But Corcovado hadn't played in over three years. They had no equipment. Not even a ball. Brad's contribution was profound and heartfelt.

Others presented gifts with great impact as well. Liz and Dan own a large goat farm in northern California. They brought animal husbandry tools and medicines for the livestock. Jeri Fujimoto, a retired youth counselor and educator, brought a wide range of crafts and origami sets. One by one, 40 American guests presented the community leadership with gifts from their hearts for the community.

Then, with cascading thumps in 2017, Trump came to Washington. Raul stepped down in Havana. Mother Nature took a big shit on Cuba on her way to Puerto Rico. All the air was let out of the balloon. And now my pool of chocolate pudding continues to slow me down and test my patience.

Yet we still want to work there. I can't believe that this blockade (we call it an embargo, Cubans call it a blockade) continues to be in place. For...no...good...reason. We imposed this cruel justice in the 1960s in the same way we now often wage war. We punish the citizens of the bad government in hopes that they will rise and revolt and overthrow their leaders. This is a strategy that has never served us well and is getting lamer as we keep employing it.

What continues to draw my attention back to this hopeless situation? All I can say is that once you go to Cuba, and you have dinner in someone's house-converted to-restaurant, and you see their pride in supporting themselves and their families, you are transformed. You watch the owner of a 1958 Chevrolet with a noisy, rattling Russian motor, proudly polishing the hood with Turtle Wax. You join hundreds on a plaza crammed to a corner where the internet is stronger trying to operate your smartphone. You watch the throngs of lovers and friends on the Malacon cooling down as the surf crashes. You spend a day at Finca Marta where Fernando and his wife prepare a luncheon from organics grown right there with a flair and passion you've never before experienced. You play a game of pickup baseball at a village. You watch the Buena Vista Social Club churn through Latin music and dance with a joy and rhythm that makes your blood pump. You light up a Romeo y Julieta and sip some rum from Cuba de Santiago and you take it all in to your core.

Thanks to new friends in Cuba on our most recent expedition, I was introduced to the original NGO in the country, Antonio Nunez Jimenez Foundation for Earth and Man. Named for the late, great scientist, explorer and humanist, this organization is like a combination of National Geographic, Nature Conservatory and Cousteau. They work as guardians of sensitive areas like caverns and wetlands and are currently developing an innovative community model for sustainability and self-sufficiency in Matanzas, Cuba. Program Director Yosiel Baez brought me to the community to meet his scientific partner Estaban Grau.

The concept of a SunSpring water plant in this community fills the bill. They want to extract water from a pre-existing well to provide a family bottle program. At just 50 cents per 20 liter bottle, they will earn over $75,000 each year to be used for further development of their ecosystem there. As of this writing, they will need to do the work on their end to obtain approvals to bring the equipment in. For our part, we'll need to work through our government to do the same. A million reasons why it should happen, and as always, many reasons it might not. Such is Cuba and the United States. But for now, I am again optimistic... with both eyes wide open.

What can I say? *We all become Cubans when we are there.* We all do the Salsa dance. But we want to change it up–two steps forward, no steps back.

WHY NOT TRY IT IN NICARAGUA?

Global Health Partners is run by a guy a lot smarter than me. With an extensive background as a news producer, including years working at CBS with Dan Rather, Bob Schwartz built strong relationships with leadership in both Cuba and Nicaragua. By the time he transitioned to starting an international relief organization, Bob chose to focus on just those two nations so desperately in need of medical supplies and pharmaceuticals. While Cuba is hard-crusted communist, Nicaragua is communist-lite, or democratic socialist. Having a strong central government with very little discretionary power available to the ministers and provincial leaders, the politicos of these two countries seem to swoon towards Venezuela and Russia with stars in their eyes. Forget that the poverty and dysfunction in all these countries make them card houses.

Bob, along with his creative and experienced cohort, Javier Bajana, have devoted decades of service in moving pharmaceuticals and medical equipment to the Cuban and Nicaraguan Health Ministries. I really can't imagine the pandemics and other health calamities that might have pounded these countries without these two men during times of global epidemics. Javier, also a news producer when he's not representing GHP in Latin America, has a journalist's drive to meet deadlines and connect all the essential players.

After we came up dry in Cuba for our efforts to install water purification solutions there, we thought we would have better luck in Nicaragua. You know something is a bit asunder in a country when you see billboards all over the cities with the smiling faces of the President and the Vice President who are married to each other. Daniel Ortega was a hero of the Sandanista revolution from 1977-1990, winning the presidency, then losing, then winning, then losing.

In power once again in 2006, Ortega brought on his wife as vice president in 2017. Rosario Murillo is a force of nature. She held the title previously in 1985, when Ortega became president the first time. Nicaraguans either love her or hate her. The Trees of Life project was Rosario's pet project to honor the 34th anniversary of the Sandanista Revolution, begun in 2013. Installing 140 abstract, brightly colored metal tree sculptures that light up at night, the artworks stand over 50 feet tall throughout Managua. With over 2.5 million bulbs, they cost a total of $1 million each year to light, and cost $25,000 each.

The 2018 protests have toppled and set fire to a number of "Rosario's trees" to demonstrate opposition to lavish government spending of the second-poorest nation in the Western Hemisphere.

The leftist Sandanistas never were big fans of the United States, as we always had propped up the predecessor, Tachito Samoza. But following the revolution, we supplied tens of millions of dollars in economic aid to the new government, more than any other country. Relations soured, however, when evidence showed that the Sandanistas supplied weapons to the leftists in El Salvador. Ortega later admitted to this, after years of denial. The Reagan Administration was fighting a proxy war with the Russians on Latin American soil and supported the Contras in a bloody civil war. But in 1987, through the deft stewardship of Democratic Speaker of the House, Jim Wright, a peace agreement was forged at a meeting of the five Central American presidents. One of those leaders was Oscar Arias of Costa Rica. He disbanded his army, with assurances of protection from the U.S., and devoted the savings towards literacy and clean water. He counseled the other countries to do the same, and for his efforts won the Nobel Prize for Peace.

In and out of power, the Ortegas always stayed involved. However, the struggling middle class and the poor were restless and oppressed. Tensions boiled over, once again in 2018, some 39 years after Ortega and his FSLN party overthrew the Samoza government for many of the issues still plaguing the country. When Ortega ordered drastic cuts in social security benefits in April, demonstrators hit the streets in the largest show of defiance in history. The government has responded in brutal fashion, with hundreds being killed and "disappeared." It is heartbreaking to see, especially since we installed a water purification system for the Health Ministry a year before and had surveyed several sites for future work. I have been most excited about the work we can do in Nicaragua, especially the prospects of establishing enterprise for the poor. But currently, Daniel Ortega and his wife are acting as brutal dictators, perhaps even worse than the Samoza dictatorship he worked so hard to overthrow many years ago.

Both Cubans and Nicaraguans have been living for generations in a sort of political soap opera, with allegiances swinging across the region and the globe to whomever will offer relief and hope. It is now in their DNA to accept a house of cards existence. When the Soviet Union collapsed in 1989, pulling all of their oil funding from Cuba, the already bankrupt nation was without food and supplies for several years. Joseph Stalin had founded the Council for Mutual Economic Assistance in 1949. COMECON was an economic organization under the leadership of the Soviet Union that comprised the countries of the Eastern Bloc along with a number of communist states elsewhere in the world. Cuba was taken into the fold in the sixties when the US embargo was imposed. With the end of the economic support, Cuba was plunged into turmoil. Ironically, the Cubans refer to that time of excruciating shortages and day-long lines as the "Special Period." This has always intrigued me about how the Cubans and other oppressed populations have used dark humor to cope with grinding suffering throughout history.

Relief, at least in the form of loans, investments and out-right grants, came in 2008 for a few years from Venezuela. Hugo Chavez had always thought of Fidel Castro as a mentor and hero. But this support and brotherhood of nations was not destined to last long. Venezuela's own economy tanked for a cascade of reasons, mostly self-imposed miscalculations by the Chavez government. Cubans today find themselves again alone, with salt being poured into the wound as the Trump Administration proceeds to roll back anything that Obama initiated, including the warming of relations.

Now let me say that I'm not an Endless Aid advocate. The H2OpenDoors project is fundamentally about self-reliance. My personal politics are more along the lines of a fiscal conservative and a social liberal. Both of our major political parties in the U.S. are, to me, feckless and corrupt. While the Facebook rants and CNN/ Fox talking heads give voice to the frustrations, I spend my time on the ground, trying to make things happen. Not because I'm a selfless person, practicing service above self. But because it drowns out the negativity and division for me. I don't want to protest about our systemic problems as much as I prefer to roll my sleeves up and do something. I've found hundreds of kindred spirits in the process. You'll not find us in a march. We're working in the trenches.

Nicaragua's Health Ministry showed more cooperation with us than Cuba as we prepared to work there in early 2017. On the far Atlantic coast of this huge nation, in the town of Puerto Cabezas, stands a crumbling hospital. The Hospital Nuevo Amancer specializes in women and child care, and it is literally crumbling. Slated for replacement by the Ortega administration with a new multimillion-dollar facility to be built nearby, no funds are sent for repairs or maintenance. In truth, it is highly unlikely that the new hospital complex will ever be built. Investments into Nicaragua's infrastructure have a habit of crumbling faster than their hospitals, roads and water systems. The much-publicized Nicaraguan Canal, to be funded by the Chinese, was to surpass the Panama Canal in terms of width and depth promising substantial wealth to the country. The new, larger super tankers would pay millions for passage. The Chinese canal project has moved to such a back burner it looks like the flame on a tiny match.

The Health Ministry jumped at our offer to fix their water problems, and little did I know how bad it was. I flew out to Managua a few months earlier, meeting Bob and Javier. We took a tiny little plane along with a couple representatives from the Health Ministry and landed an hour later on a dirt field in Puerto Cabezas.

Once a vibrant fishing village, we were picked up by the staff, and upon arrival at the hospital I was dumbstruck. The first thing

I saw was a large rusted and abandoned media stack that had been installed long ago. These were large white, square tanks contained in metal cages. The raw well water would be pumped through the media in these tanks for rudimentary purification. Some might contain bio sand, others chlorine. The problem with these systems is that the villages often can't replace the media once it has been used. The religious organization that had installed the system had long ago moved on to install over 5000 of these stacks worldwide. The empty system had been sitting disconnected for the previous four years, according to the hospital administrator. He handed me the lab analysis of the well water that I had asked for prior to leaving the States. On the second page, in the section I always go to first, were the worst numbers I had ever seen. Total coliform was 990 and E.coli counts were over 550. Counts should be zero. This means that the well water was extraordinarily toxic with bacteria. Back home, we hear about an E.coli outbreak occasionally associated with a lettuce recall or a few Chipotle restaurants. This is the particular bacterial strain that is fecal coliform, and it can cause serious issues. When E.coli is present, you can be sure there are additional pathogens, and so the total coliform count gives us the fuller picture. The Nicaraguan hospital's counts would have been worse than those toxic Superfund sites we became familiar with in the 80s.

The administrator was smiling as I read the report. "Excuse me, but did you read this report?" I asked. "Your water is poison." He answered, with a shrug, in Spanish, "Vienen enfermos, los enfermamos mas." *They come in sick, we get them sicker.* The municipal well was the cause of the contamination, I surmised. Built dozens of years earlier, the casing had probably fractured, allowing the seepage of soil contaminants into the water supply during every rain event.

I just couldn't believe it. Surely, they had to be doing something about the water these past four years. He brought us to the operating room, a busy section in bad need of a paint job and better equipment. The water at the sink is put into a pitcher, then poured into what looks like a pottery vessel placed on top of another pitcher. This method, they were hopeful, would remove much of the bacteria from their raw source. Ceramic, porous water filters like this are very popular with academics and well-meaning yet uninformed volunteers. The attraction to use these products is that they can be made locally from easily-sourced material. The problem is that they turn out to do more harm than good. Made from clay, straw and a little silver, the water percolates through the porous material. Drinking water stored in clay pots has been a method used for thousands of years. However, no one ever effectively cleans these pots, which build up with bacterial and viral contaminants like a science fair exhibit. The hospital simply would replace these earthen filter pots every few months. "How do you know it's time to replace them?" I asked. "When they get a little slimy," was the answer.

Bob and I sat down with the administrator and department heads. I drew out a schematic of what we will contribute and install in three months' time. First, I explained that we will bring a proper pump to send the well water up to the elevated tank on the property. (The current one in the pump house was sending a mini-Bellagio fountain out through its cracked casing.) Next, we would re-route the drain of the tank directly to the SunSpring and purify the water to the quality of the US EPA standards, removing all the bacteria and viruses. Next, we would lay pipe from the SunSpring to the operating room and to the kitchen that would send purified water to those two essential places. Finally, we would provide 20 water coolers with five-gallon bottles to be placed all around the hospital for drinking. The staff would keep the bottles filled at all times directly from the SunSpring.

A few months later, we arrived back in Nicaragua with a group of 14 adventurers, and we spent two days with installation and training. As luck would have it, we performed this work in a small monsoon, drenched to our tightie-whities. But we got it done, and we solved their issue—for the time being. On a follow-up inspection trip six months later, the cistern holding the well water was severely cracking, and everywhere we looked we saw disrepair. The hospital is decomposing every day, with no federal funding to fix anything. We solved a problem for the women and children of Puerto Cabezas, but everything around our solution is caving in. I can only find solace in the saying, "Perfect is the enemy of good." At least they're not drinking a bacterial cocktail any more or using infected water in surgeries. But it's hard to be proud of a contribution of money, time and effort when the squalor continues.

When our team returned to Managua, we visited a delightful organization called Los Pipitos. As soon as we walked into their central campus, our spirits were lifted. Ruth Elizondo, the determined co-founder and treasurer, had us sit down in the general assembly room for a special presentation by the clients. Dozens of young people, most with Down syndrome, some with mild cerebral palsy and others either deaf or visually-impaired, performed a series of dances. Colorful costumes and a narrator explained the customary, Nicaraguan ritual dances of cultural significance. We had brought with us piles of cognitive development toys and tools which were laid on tables around us. We experienced the warmth and the humor of these people, ages 6 to 35.

Ruth was a Health Ministry executive 30 years prior when she gave birth to two twin boys, both with Down syndrome. There was nothing that the Ministry could do to help. So, she started Los Pipitos with her meager salary as she started to meet other parents in similar situations. Today, in more than 80 facilities, the organization works with over 15,000 families coming from all over Nicaragua, and many from neighboring countries. For the past 17 years, the center's primary source of funding has been a TV telethon every year. The 36-hour broadcast was watched throughout Nicaragua.

Los Pipitos would raise over $1 million from corporate and individual pledges called in, Jerry Lewis Muscular Dystrophy-style. Upon our visit, however, Ruth told us of a breaking development. "I have sued the two men who have run the Telethon Foundation all these years," Ruth told me in a hushed tone. When she had asked why the center only sees $400,000 per year and wondered what happens with the other $600,000, the men abruptly cancelled future telethons. The most popular charity in Nicaragua was being swindled, and Rose brought them to court. The Ministry of the Interior ordered the Telethon to release all of the funds it had recently collected, but a light bulb went off in my head. Or at least a faucet opened.

I explained to Ruth that we had just installed a SunSpring on the eastern coast. There was a modified version IWT was developing at one-third of the cost called the WallSpring. It was appropriate for urban environments where there was reliable electrical power and municipal water pressure. We could install three of these into your main centers throughout the city, purify the water and fill five-gallon family bottles. Label them as Los Pipitos water, indicating that all of the net profits go to support the organization. Each plant, at capacity, would produce over $150,000 in revenue. That's a total of $450,000 in annual earnings from water sales. The bottling and sales would be handled by your clients and staff, and the sales would be run by your two sons, now 30 years old. Even with their obvious Down's affliction, they seemed quite capable and were very outgoing. What better pitchmen than them?

Ruth was over the moon. All the funding lost from the cancellation of the Telethon would be replaced by money they earned through their own water enterprise. We would have to wait until the legal matters were settled, however. The Telethon guys were claiming that they had rights to all of the organization's property. Then Ortega's actions set the country on a path towards civil war that we are faced with now. I don't know if our plan for Los Pipitos will ever take life. And I don't know how long the hospital in Puerto Cabezas can stand on its own foundations. When you're a water warrior, you have to be a bit like Sisyphus rolling the boulder up the hill, watching it roll down again, and rolling up over and over and over. The difference is that we haven't been sentenced to the futility by the Lord of the Underworld. At least I haven't gotten that memo yet.

HOW DO WE CHOOSE WHERE TO WORK?

As you might imagine, there is no shortage of places that we could install a safe water plant. Rotary International conventions and district meetings are a continual source of village and school intel where we might be able to leverage big impact with frugal funding. As we perform our installations, we also do site surveys for future installations. After all, we prefer to have clusters of water plants in regions and countries throughout the world for efficiency and efficacy. Our second expedition to Nepal was a typical case where we installed a third SunSpring water system, bringing 18 adventurers to help us, followed by a four-day trek through the Annapurna Mountains in the Himalayans.

We had put in two systems in a couple villages in the eastern province the year before, following one of their frequent earthquakes. Narayan Shrestha was introduced to me by Dr. Andrew Lustig, founder of Global Outreach Doctors. I had met Andrew in the Philippines during the aftermath of Super Typhoon Yolanda. Narayan lives in Boulder, Colorado with his wife, and was born and raised in Nepal. Narayan was an entrepreneur from an early age. By the time I first met him, he had put 90 of his family members into business in the United States and Canada, all selling Nepalese goods. Chances are if you've wandered into a store with Nepalese folk art, Buddhist knick-knacks, and the colorful fabrics of the region, it is owned by one of Narayan's family members.

Each year, in Boulder, Narayan puts on a fundraiser for his Helping Hands USA organization, raising funds for a number of schools and hospitals they have organized in Nepal. Jack and I, along with a Rotarian friend, Bob McKinley, traveled to Nepal with Narayan to put in SunSprings not long after the recent spate of quakes. A secondary school in Khandbari, Narayan's hometown, and Chainpur, a village across a great gorge were the recipients. The mountains of Nepal make the Rocky Mountains seem like gentle, rolling hills. Majestic and aggressive, the higher peaks, like Everest and Annapurna, pierce the sky and change the weather to their liking. A flight from Kathmandu to Khandbari takes about 30 minutes. By car, nine hours along hairpin turns that look from the air like the finest filigree on ancient ornamentation. More often than not, flights are cancelled due to storms and winds within the mountains not evident at all in the big city.

Arriving with Narayan in his hometown is like accompanying a returning king. His entire 4'11" frame seemed to stretch with a regal gate as he walked the dirt streets greeting well-wishers.

Narayan's Surya Secondary School is a boarding school during the semesters for 900 children. Water comes from surging underground rivers, coursing through the granite of the Himalayans, with very occasional outlets or water points. Students would fill reused Coke bottles from their main water point, a hike of about one-quarter mile...vertical, down then back up. The water was crystal clear, yet contaminated from bacterial infiltration, according to the lab report we had received a month previous. We tapped into a source and installed the SunSpring at the school, uphill from the cafeteria, sending the purified water down by gravity to a web of pipes feeding the sinks. Safe drinking water now serves all the students and will shortly be provided to the public.

Narayan's business sense immediately recognized opportunity in the provisioning of water in this location. A new road had been started to connect Nepal with China, a mere mile from the school gates. He has acquired blow molding machinery to create his own large family bottles to contain and sell the purified water. Narayan is one of those characters that I describe as a "force of nature." Boundless enthusiasm and energy, he provides enough inspiration to turn his vision into reality. Thomas Edison has said that "vision, without execution, is hallucination." Narayan makes his dreams real, benefitting thousands upon thousands.

After a second install in Chainpur, in the middle of a cornfield, I learned what Narayan's strategy was there. This village of 1000 farmers wanted to start a water sales business to fund the building of a badly-needed health clinic. Narayan offered to go 50-50 on construction. The town would sell their bottled water and contribute funding for the clinic to be matched by Narayan's personal contribution. I learned that in a poor country like Nepal, the greatest benefactors and social innovators are their own citizens who have left, become educated in Western universities, created wealth, and return to give back. It turns out that some Nepalese that never left are mired in cynicism and jealousy of those that did and succeeded. When I meet Nepalese Rotarians at a Rotary convention and I show them photos of what we do in Nepal, they roll their eyes at the name, Narayan Shrestha. "He should come back and donate his wealth, not profit from it in Nepal." I couldn't disagree more. Countries like Nepal should celebrate and honor people like Narayan. The schools and hospitals he has built employ and train hundreds for solid careers in health and education. Reliance on the government or donations cripple the ability for a middle class to grow and thrive. Pick any nation on Earth where you have the very rich, and the very poor making up the majority of the population, and you'll find an overly-controlling central government and a steady influx of charitable welfare contributions. Those countries don't run very well and generational poverty continues to grind on.

The following year, we returned to Kathmandu with Narayan to install a SunSpring on the roof of the brand-new Helping Hands Hospital. On a previous trip, I was toured through the old hospital down the street. This was where I had encountered all those folks in pre-op for stone removal procedures. The new facility towers at seven floors and was 90% complete when we developed the purified water program. A large underground cistern for the hospital receives continual municipal well water. Highly contaminated, we installed a solar pump to send the water up to a large retaining tank on the roof. From there, the SunSpring processes the raw water and sends it out to six smaller roof tanks which, in turn, gravity feed the contents down to each floor of the hospital. When we met with the US Embassy in Kathmandu, the director of water and sanitation told us that the hospital would be only the second building in the entire city with purified water available at every sink, every faucet, even every toilet as we enjoy in the USA. "What was the first building?" I asked. "The US Embassy!" she responded, smiling with arms outstretched.

Jon's sister Jaye halfway through her 4-year battle with ovarian cancer

Jaye passed away in 2009, four years before the start of H2OpenDoors

Our very first installation in Huyajakan, a Lahu hilltribe village near the Myanmar border in 2013

Training of village technicians on the five basic monthly maintenance procedures

The taste of the water needs to be as good or better than bottled water

High School students join the
H2OpenDoors project, and
get some local coverage

Students gain a unique
perspective from our
expeditions to Mexico

With former Mexican President
Vicente Fox at CentroFox

The first water at Cd. Guzman
in Jalisco state, Mexico

We asked this girl how far the water point was, and she told us 3 miles each way

Our Haitian NGO partners on the mayor's balcony

Tacloban from the air after Supertyphoon Yolanda caused a 23-foot wave, sweeping thousands into the sea to their death

Behind Jon are 700 filled white body bags. The eventual total was 7000 bodies recovered

Even in the most desperate of conditions, a child's laughter rings out

Tanzania 2018-Jon addresses 90,000 Busiya tribe members with Chief Makwaia looking on

The 7Saba festival in Shinyanga, Tanzania, draws nearly 100,000, with traditional dances, music and warrior games

Labels in Swahili let residents of Nhobola village know that this water is purified, delivered right to their huts each week

Training day in Shinyanga, TZ with RACHEL, Remote Access Community Hotspot for Education & Learning

Umra Omar, founder of Safari Doctors and UN Person of the Year with Mai Water, the water brand being sold from The SunSpring bottling plant to support the medical teams serving the archipelago off Kenya's coast.

Our Masai partners in the Mara, Amos and Harris

Keith Marsh performing his photographic magic on our safari

Shortly after Hurricane Maria devastated Puerto Rico in 2017, H2OpenDoors established a purification plant in the hardest-hit town of Punta Santiago

Darrell Ransom is Director of Logistics for FEMA. After visiting with Jack Barker in Washington in August 2018, Mr. Ransom traveled to Puerto Rico and viewed one of the SunSprings in full swing. He knew how ludicrous it is to provide bottled water long-term for communities.

2 weeks after the Director's visit, aerial images of 20,000 pallets left abandoned on a runway in Puerto Rico hit the Internet. Actual cost of $7 million, degrading and wasting away in the hot sun for several months. Mr. Ransom no doubt was aware of the folly and irresponsibility when he viewed the SunSpring as an alternative to the madness.

Michelle Nirenstein and Jon Kaufman live together in San Carlos, California. Their three grown children are out of the house, replaced by three dogs.

VOODOO ON
GOOD FRIDAY

When Jack called me about going to Haiti in 2015, I jumped on it. He hadn't been back there since the five months he spent in 2010 after the earthquake. And my only experience, of course, was when I made The Big Vow to my sister as we watched Haitians pour into Labadie to glean from the trash cans after our feast.

Les Irois (pronounced *lazy wah*) is that part of the island on the farthest west point, looking like a finger pointing out towards Jamaica and Guantanamo, Cuba. Arriving in Port-au-Prince, Jack and I met his technician, Harry. Short, black as coal, with an infectious smile that lights up a room, Harry had been shadowing Jack during the quake's aftermath. He was a mechanical engineer who, as did countless others, lost employment in all the destruction. Harry was fascinated with the SunSpring and became Jack's constant companion, protector, translator and assistant. With over 60 SunSprings spread out all over the island today, Harry is the head technician keeping them humming.

When we arrived back in Haiti, Harry met us at the airport in his official SunSpring truck, a yellow four-seater Toyota pickup with the SunSpring logos emblazoned on the doors. In the truck bed sat the thousand-pound crate, strapped in, hanging over the open gate by about two feet. We were to begin our 14-hour drive, immediately, out to Les Irois.

"The good news is that I have a spare tire," Harry informed us as we navigated through jammed traffic of the capitol city. "What's the bad news?" I inquired. Harry said, "I don't have a jack or lug wrench." While this was disconcerting, I understood his anxiety about two hours into the ride as the roads turned into deep-rutted, rocky dirt trails.

It was Good Friday, and in a voodoo culture like Haiti, they have mixed elements of Catholic ceremonies with voodoo rituals. Dating back to the 17th century when colonists brought African slaves to Haiti, Rara groups were a major form of expression. Rara (pronounced *rah-rah*) is mostly party and parade with participants dressed in colorful costumes, many carrying sticks and musical instruments, singing and dancing. Each group usually has a cylindrical crude bamboo trumpet called a vaksen. Setting a monotonous, repeating rhythm, the sound seems to induce a trance within the other sounds of drums, whistles, bells and Creole chants. Most are peaceful and entertaining to watch as we drove the roads. The leaders of the groups carry a voodoo flag at the front, and guide everyone to the side of the road to allow cars to pass. But something sinister starts to happen as the day creeps towards dusk. Could be that the revelers have been enjoying moonshine, or that they are drunk on voodoo. After driving through these scenes for over seven hours, we approached the rear of a very large Rara. As Harry slowed down and moved to the left of the road, the group didn't move to the right to allow our passing. Soon we were surrounded, the music stopped and it became strangely quiet.

The leader stood directly in front of our truck, eyes fixated on Harry, then me in the shotgun seat. It was a standoff, except it was way past High Noon. I've learned a simple technique whenever threatened. Don't make direct eye contact. Instead, look over the aggressor's left shoulder. Really throws them off and makes them slightly paranoid about what might be coming up their flank. So this was the position I took the entire time. After five of the longest minutes I've ever experienced, the leader raised both of his arms to the sky and crossed them in an "X." *What the hell does that mean?*

I flashed to horror stories I had heard, like the Haitian Necklace. That's where they put a gasoline-soaked tire around you and light it on fire. Or use machetes in creative ways. As I was wishing my loved ones goodbye in my mental text messages, the crowd parted, the leader stepped out of the way, and we slowly drove down the road. Turning a bend in the road, not even a mile away from that scene, we heard a loud BANG! The right rear tire had exploded from a sharp rock in the road. The three of us looked at each other, realizing the dread and remembering that we had no way to change the tire.

We scrambled out to first check that the crate was still attached. Then we saw the shredded tire and bent rim. An old Buick approached, and we flagged it over, all the while sure that the Rara group would also be approaching soon. We asked to borrow their jack, and they graciously helped to remove it from their car. I also took their lug wrench and realized immediately that it wouldn't fit the smaller bolts on the Toyota. By this time, we were joined by several locals offering their assistance. And then that group grew to a dozen. One of the men suggested we use the jack to lift the truck while he tries to find a suitable tool to remove the bolts. After 30 minutes of waiting for his return, with the Toyota perched on three tires and a jack, we flagged down a Toyota sedan. Overjoyed at our good fortune, we asked for his lug wrench. Amazingly, the Raras never showed up behind us. But we had another issue with over 12 Haitian men surrounding us again, all claiming their part in our rescue. I gave a $20 bill to the apparent leader, asking him to share it. This caused shoving and spitting amongst them. I pulled out 10 singles, handed it out to some of the others while I motioned to Harry and Jack to get in the truck and start driving. Running towards the open passenger door, my body straining to make the leap, we heard another loud crash.

The tailgate, holding part of the crate, had fallen off. Fallen off! Our "helpers" were back for round two. Harry and I assessed the situation, determined that the crate was still secure, and loaded the tailgate into the bed. We were off again to complete our journey.

As the sun set and the full moon rose over the mountainous terrain, we had only two more hours until arriving in Les Irois. We passed through a small village with neat rows of middle-class bungalows along the road. The bright full moon and our headlights revealed that we were driving over hundreds of palm fronds, which we thought odd.

As we ascended a steep climb over what would be the last range of mountains before the coastal towns of west Haiti, we witnessed the strangest of all Rara groups. Marching down the hill in tight formation, a group of about a dozen men in army-like fatigues brandishing machetes eerily smiled and chanted in the moonlight. As we passed them, their eyes fixed ahead, we just shook our heads. "Well that happened," Jack finally said.

Pulling into the town of Les Irois, literally the end of the road in Haiti, we were greeted by Winsor, the head of an NGO and the most respected citizen of the region. More of a mayor, Winsor and his family lived in comparably luxurious digs. His posse was equally welcoming, and we felt instantly safe and at home. Winsor's young, beautiful wife plied us with drinks and showed us to our rooms on the second floor of their house.

It was after 10PM, and I needed a shower. The house was brand new, and the shower was magnificent. Until you realized there was no running water. Instead, two buckets sat near the drain. One was full, presumably of harvested rainwater. The other was empty. I tried to get clean using these tools as best as I could.

Jack had traveled to Les Irois five years before when he first met Winsor and his team. He had been telling me that this is the most beautiful place I would ever experience. They had been asking him for five years to return and help them with their water problem. Cut off from the rest of Haiti, it is near impossible to have regular deliveries of supplies, like safe drinking water. When we arrived, everyone was wearing dark gray t-shirts with the name of their NGO and the title "Welcome Jack Baker" back to Les Irois. We didn't have the heart to tell them his last name is Barker.

The next morning, we gathered for breakfast out by the beach at Winsor's father's house. Everywhere you go in this town of 8,000, surrounded by another 20,000, you see conch shells. One of the most prolific spots on Earth for conch, it is served in every meal and provides landscaping decoration. Turns out that harvesting the shells in the Caribbean Sea is their form of the lottery. In one out of an estimated 10,000 of the Queen conch, a pearl is formed. The deep-pink conch pearls can fetch between $2000 and $30,000 per carat.

As we sat in the elder's front garden, listening to the surf and watching the conch farmers repair their nets, I couldn't help but feel I was in a paradise far from the suffering and poverty. It was idyllic. Cut off from the rest of the island, they were only getting two hours of electricity a week. Winsor and the other privileged residents had generators. One of his kids, a delightful little girl, climbed onto his lap as we conversed. We were about to go over to one of the schools to install the SunSpring fed off of a hand-dug well they prepared for our arrival. His wife came out and presented Jack and me with custom-made coffee cups *with our photos on them* pouring us Haitian-grown coffee. I was astounded at how industrious they were. With the cherubic daughter smiling, I asked my habitually inappropriate question, "Winsor, have you had health issues with the very young and the very old due to the water quality?" "Yes, Mr. Jon. Last year we had 55 children die of a cholera outbreak," Windsor said, clutching tighter to his baby girl. We all sat in silence dealing with that awful reality.

We strolled through the town center, all the way being welcomed by children also walking to the school. "Blanc, blanc!" they would shout out and giggle. Jack and I are true oddballs in this town of Haitians cut off from everything. Adorable kids would run up and grab our hands, look at the contrast of their skin and ours, and start laughing as we strolled. They would tap each other out so that more had the opportunity to walk hand in hand with the strange white visitors.

We were halfway done with the SunSpring installation in the school's quad when someone came running into the compound asking Harry if they could borrow his truck. A man had walked all night *with a machete blade in his eye socket.* He had heard that an ambulance was at Les Irois, and they could take him to the nearby town of Jeremie's emergency hospital. By the time he arrived at Les Irois, he was near death. The ambulance had been recently donated, but no one had a key. So, Harry's SunSpring truck was the only other choice. A mattress was thrown into the truck bed, and six others accompanied the victim in the back, with Harry at the wheel.

We completed the installation, and Winsor and the elders conducted a prayer circle around it, complete with Haitian songs and Christian hymns. Voodoo and Christianity coexist in harmony in this community, especially on Easter weekends. Later in the afternoon, as we gathered on Winsor's deck overlooking the main village street, we shared cold beer and cigars. I had four cigars with me and cut them up into 12 little stogies, passing them out to the team. Most had never smoked a cigar, saying it was a rich man's vice. "Well, better start diving for conch!" I joked. We all had a good belly laugh, and then heard the generator shut down and saw lights go on.

The two-hour electricity ration had begun for Les Irois. Soon, dozens were running up the street, from both directions. Across from Winsor's house, a smaller bungalow had a luxury item that everyone knew about...a 13" Sony color TV. The island's most popular soap opera, *Destinee*, was just coming on. The weekly series follows the joys and sorrows of Moira, a young girl from the provinces who finds love and betrayal in Port au Prince. Almost 100 people were gathered outside the window of the home, peering in to watch, having a grand old time. A Haitian drive-in movie, except on foot. The festive atmosphere, the idyllic evening weather, the sound of the surf and warmth of our hosts made this day one of the happiest and fulfilling I can remember.

Harry joined us later and reported, sadly, that the man had died at the hospital. The machete attack was the work of that military-like Rara group. We sat in stunned silence as Harry was filling us in. "The poor man owned one of the bungalows in the village we had passed. Several of the residents went out to confront the group and asked them to stop chopping on their palm trees." They were attacked. I wondered what would have transpired had we arrived at that town two hours earlier as the homeowners were confronting the marauders. We would have surely joined the fight. The tire fiasco was probably divine intervention.

SECOND RESPONDERS MATTER

FINDING ANSWERS

In my year-long pursuit of technologies to purify water, I read everything I could get my hands on, spoke to everyone I could who knew the issues, and visited several factories. Turns out the Godfather of Research in this area is a guy named Frantisek Kozisek. Dr. Kozisek is the longtime head of the Department of Water Health in the Czech Republic. Exhaustive studies and extensive peer-reviewed papers issued by his department form the basis of public drinking water programs throughout the world. His takeaway cautions often surround the debate about whether demineralized water is healthy or not. He warns that the evidence is clear. Artificial removal of toxins, along with essential minerals from water through reverse-osmosis and distillation, can present adverse health effects to those who drink this "empty" water every day.

He writes:

"The potential for adverse health effects from long term consumption of demineralized water is of interest not only in countries lacking adequate fresh water, but also in countries where some types

of home water treatment systems are widely used or where some types of bottled water are consumed."

This excerpt from an exhaustive paper became the primary guidance I used to focus my search for appropriate technology. Water devoid of essential minerals and electrolytes is extraordinarily unhealthy. I was already convinced that reverse osmosis systems were too wasteful of the raw water, in short supply in most places. But it also opened up my eyes about all forms of distillation and potential risks to health and pipes due to inconsistencies at the utility level. Popular at the time, but since gone into the shadows, was Dean Kamen and his invention called the Slingshot. A vapor compression distiller, this portable unit was featured in magazines from *Popular Science* and *Time*. After all, Kamen is a prolific inventor. From the creation of an improved stent for cardiovascular surgeries to the Segway, Kamen has been trumpeted as the Edison of our times.

Having great respect for men like Dean Kamen, I was intrigued when Coca-Cola adopted the Slingshots as their primary method to provide purified water to the rural poor throughout their wide footprint of service. At least two of Coke's annual reports devoted multiple pages to photos and copy of this initiative. In a TED-Med presentation in 2010, Kamen explained that his company, DEKA, had developed a system with some amazing benefits, turning contaminated water (even human urine) into safe drinking water. The presentation's bullet points included:

- five years of operation without overhaul or maintenance
- uses less than a kilowatt of power (lower than the power consumption of a microwave oven)
- generates 1000 liters of pure water/day, enough for 100 people for hygiene and cooking
- meets the U.S. pharmacopoeia standard for water for injections

- requires no pre-treatment, pipelines, engineers, consumables (osmosis membranes, charcoal, etc.), or installation permits

The idea here was not particularly new. Boil water, capture the steam, condense and dispense distilled water. I had already determined that distilled water, void of any essential minerals, was a direction I wanted to avoid. I was also unimpressed with the amount of water produced at capacity. One thousand liters a day simply wasn't sufficient if I wanted to work with large populations at a time AND guide them towards starting a water sales business. But what really troubled me was the power consumption necessary to boil water, and the math. The acquisition cost of the Slingshot, plus the power requirements, divided by the at-capacity output of water over the course of a year was far more than what a village should pay. More than what donors ought to pay as well. Cheaper to just send flats of bottled water to the village every few days.

Each week, it seems, we hear of a new device. Lately, the media has been gaga over technology that captures water out of the air. Atmospheric Water Generators, as this class of equipment is called, have been tempting the thirsty for a couple generations. The truth about these "new" ideas is the limited scale, and the fact that any process that condenses water from air will entrain contaminants into a concentrate. So, it becomes necessary to filter this water before it can be consumed by humans.

Most of the devices du jour are ones best used for a weekend hike through Yosemite, not as a permanent water solution for villages, hospitals and schools. I've previously mentioned the LifeStraw. This device and others that have a charcoal plug have never claimed to remove viral toxins. They can be moderately effective for cysts, parasites and most bacteria, but they require periodic replacement of the carbon filter and extensive cleaning. The charcoal insert can become a bit of a science experiment, growing cultures of bacteria, defeating the purpose of the unit. Newer variations of the device contain a bundle of 0.02 micron hollow fiber membrane strands. The membranes at this pore size also do nothing about viruses. By contrast, the pore size in the membranes contained in a SunSpring are 0.05 micron, smaller than a human-harmful virus.

Squat in a river and suck out water through the Straw. Use it straight out of the box, and for several days, or even weeks, you can rest assured that you won't ingest bacteria or protozoan cysts. That's the good news. Use it much longer, and there's a good chance you'll be sucking through a device that is actually growing these contaminants inside its plastic housing. But the biggest concern to me is that millions of people, using this "solution," are doing absolutely nothing to prevent the ingestion of multi-syllable viruses. Over a hundred species that cause hepatitis, gastroenteritis, meningitis and conjunctivitis are welcomed into your throat and gut with these camping gadgets.

I ask again, *would you want to have your grandmother use these items as her way to drink safe drinking water?*

There was one other aspect that troubled me. Ethics. Widely distributed, CEO Mikkel Vestergaard Frandsen invested over $30 million of his own money to manufacture these devices and distribute in a business model copied years later by Toms shoes. Buy one, and we'll give a free one to the poor. In this case, there was a cynical profit motive that twisted me up. As reported in 2011 in the Stanford Social Innovation Review, Vestergaard Frandsen's Carbon for Water project gave a million LifeStraws out to families in Kenya...for free. By convincing the certification group, The Gold Standard, that Life Straws prevent the need for Kenyans to boil their water, carbon credits could be earned. And because this was in Kenya, the bogus notion that everyone was boiling their water, shockingly, earned certification from The Gold Standard board, allowing these credits to be sold at a premium. Vestergaard Frandsen earned millions of dollars selling these credits to countries with caps and exchanges on their carbon releases.

Forget that there was never any solid evidence of a statistically significant reduction in diarrheal disease. Breathless media and academic advocates of the latest gadget on the scene cause us to lose valuable time. Every day, thousands are dying from bad water. When I first joined Rotary in 2012, Life Straws were being bought by Rotary clubs in lots of thousands at $25 each. I knew that this was worse than naive. It was doing absolutely nothing, other than providing a phantom sense of helping.

A POND OF CRITTERS AND SUPER TYPHOON YOLANDA

Our maiden installations were at two hill tribes in the Chiang Mai province of Northern Thailand, near the Myanmar border. Peter and Jennifer Katz, dear friends, joined us on our very first outing and our work started and completed all on February 3, 2013. I remember the exact date, because our San Francisco 49ers were facing off against the Baltimore Ravens in Super Bowl XLVII. We tried to keep our phones off. The time zone difference meant that any of our friends back home could spoil the results. We were looking forward to getting back to Chiang Mai that evening to watch a replay at a fun British pub.

Funds of over $50,000 were raised at an H2OpenDoors Party a few months earlier for the purchase of two SunSpring systems. My friend, Danny Navarro, and I went to the factory in Colorado to learn how to install and configure the systems. We headed to Thailand with a dozen friends including two students from Redwood High, our local continuation high school in Redwood City, California.

Smack dab in the center of Silicon Valley, Noah and Bethany had never been on an airplane, much less across the Pacific Ocean.

High school students have been on several of our expeditions. They add a fun element, with energy and humor. In Noah and Bethany's case, they were the "winners" of a contest in their Green Academy class at Redwood High. All the students studied about water, various technologies and about Northern Thailand, and had to write a paper and present it to us. These two were the best and they worked really hard all semester. Once we had arrived at the village of Huayjakan, Noah asked, "I'm thirsty. Where's the drinking fountains?" "Have you learned nothing, grasshopper?" I chided him. "We are here because they have no drinking water." We teased poor Noah all week. Redwood High students come from East Palo Alto and live in poverty. But when they see what true poverty looks like, they get a sense of perspective. To not have the most basic of human needs was a stunning wake up call. Before long, as they both mingled with their peers in the village, I started noticing that they were teaching them gang signs. Wait, what? Turned out that they were communicating our mantra: Water, Education, Peace. "W" with three fingers up. "E" with those three fingers turned sideways. "P" with two fingers up in the victory/peace salute. Each signal they would say Water...Education...Peace. The Thai kids were repeating, but in the Thai language. They were teaching each other their languages! All over the village, kids were doing the gang signing for the three days we were there. You gotta love it!

For our first installs I wanted baselines. In pursuit of data that would serve as Proof of Concept, I created a survey card with the assistance of faculty at Stanford Medical School. There were seven questions, but the first one was the most important: "*How many times in the past two weeks did you have an episode of diarrhea?*"

This bank of questions was posed to 10% of the population of Huayjakan village. Made up of 2500 Lisu and Lahu hill tribe people, the community relied on a spring-fed pond installed two years before by Engineers Without Borders. The water in the pond tested high in E.coli bacteria. The survey was administered to 250 random residents with great sensitivity and privacy by the Rotary clubs of Northern Thailand and the village elders in order to determine the effects of the bacterial contamination that showed up in the lab analysis.

It turned out that on installation day, the survey had showed 70 people reporting multiple bouts of diarrhea in the previous 14 days, or 28% of the population. Five months later, the Rotary clubs conducted the same surveys with another 250 residents. The results were astonishing–a 76% reduction in the incidents of diarrhea. The only factor that changed for them was the access to safe drinking water. We did not address sanitation (there was open defecation) or hygiene (no soap at the village). This codified for me that we were on the correct path, and that the SunSpring was the best and least expensive answer to serve the largest number of people.

While my Proof of Concept gave me confidence, I wasn't sure about throwing another big fundraising gala when we returned stateside. Our Northern Thailand Rotary friends were pleading with us to go just across the border with them in a few months. Myanmar, formerly Burma, was awakening from decades of autocratic rule and drug cartel influence. Rotary had been banned in that country, and the lure to help them with water quality was too much to resist.

So, we threw another party. It was November of 2013, and our catered Burmese food and special guests from that country helped to create an understanding of the challenges and the hope we could bring. I came to the stage, grabbed the microphone, thanked the band, the caterers, the poker dealers and bartenders. I had an important announcement to make to the 200 guests. CNN News had been reporting that the largest typhoon in recorded history turned the town of Tacloban, Philippines into a wasteland. A 23-foot wave had engulfed the harbor, drawing thousands of families into the ocean to their deaths.

"I wonder if I can suggest a pivot, tonight," I began. "We all assembled here to learn about the struggle in Myanmar. But the Philippines has just been hit hard. Can we help Myanmar at a later date and provide relief for our Filipino friends and families now?" Everyone had been watching the news of the growing typhoon for a couple days. This was a perfect decision to them. Applause, thumbs in the air, tears running down cheeks, we pivoted.

A few days later, I was invited to speak to the Santa Cruz Rotary club. Jim Zenner, a new friend, had been a solid Rotarian for 30 years. His niece had recently written a book called *Just Water*. Christiana Peppard discusses the ethics of water and all that it entails in this short but powerful book. I had met her at a conference a few months prior, and she, in turn, said I would enjoy meeting Uncle Jim. Since then, Jim Zenner and I are like brothers. At his Rotary meeting, following my presentation about the Philippines, a dozen members lined up to hand me envelopes of cash and checks, much like it was at my bar mitzvah. The support from this group was truly moving, and in following years, we've formed quite a coalition in Latin America. We ultimately raised $105,000 for the Philippines.

Two weeks later, Jack Barker and I went on our first trip together, boarding a Philippines Airlines flight out of SFO.

The first four weeks after a major disaster is considered the "window for first response." Our shipment of 2,000-pound crates to Cebu was accomplished for free by a rapid response team out of Florida. We arrived at Cebu's airport, which had suffered mild damage, as it was a few hundred miles to the west of the hardest hit Eastern Visayas. C-130 transports lined the airfield, and large signs pointed us to the One Stop Shop of government representatives. Well organized at a dozen tables, each ministry of government was present for us to move through clearances and questioning. Even though all paperwork was produced by pen rather than computer, we spent only about 45 minutes at five tables.

We were asked who we were, and what help were we providing. All satisfied, we were brought to our hosts, waiting for us outside. We were to leave the next day for Tacloban, the capital of the island Leyte. Birth home of Imelda Romualdez Marcos, Tacloban took the largest brunt of the disaster. That evening, we met with our hosts from the Methodist Adventist Hospital system in Cebu. Benot Blase is the enthusiastic chaplain for the hospital and served as our guide for the entire trip. He arranged every meeting and moved us through every bureaucratic challenge as we entered Tacloban.

Normal routes and transportation methods were shut down. Everywhere we looked, as we travelled from Cebu to the nearest coast of neighboring Leyte, was an ever-growing view of damage. We had to drive for nine hours to the east coast for Tacloban. Power poles were at 60-degree angles with some still sparking. Roofs were twisted off of structures, strewn blocks away. But the scene was bone-chilling as we arrived at night into the town. With no street lights, the highway entering Tacloban was only illuminated by our truck's headlamps. Sitting alongside the road, on both sides, were hundreds of men, women and kids staring into the void. They had burned all of the available wood the previous three weeks just sitting there waiting the night out. Pitch black. Empty stares. Trauma.

We pulled up to the RTR Hospital, one of two hospitals in town still operating. We bunked down on the floor of one of the upstairs classrooms. This hospital, owned by the Romualdez family, served as a multi-care facility and a widely respected medical university. The next morning, we met aid workers from a dozen countries. Teams with cadaver dogs came and went in their daily search for bodies in the rubble. Our crates were there waiting for us. But no Rotary club members. Rotary, along with thousands of others in town, had been evacuated to Manila. Our partners on this project were to be the hospital staff members. So, we got to work.

Directly in front of the emergency room, we took over the parking space of the hospital's administrator to install the SunSpring. Tapping off of the municipal water feed going to the hospital, we hooked up the SunSpring to return purified water to the hospital's primary care rooms and to a faucet available on the side of the unit. Within 30 minutes of the completion of our installation, the word was out. Hundreds of people brought any container they could find to fill up with safe water. There never was safe drinking water in the town, and the hospital often used bottled water for wound cleansing and emergency patients. But after the typhoon, the pumps to the town's web of pipes were often turned off for lack of diesel fuel. By the time we were there, pumps were restored thanks to the efforts of Philip Romualdez, nephew of Imelda Marcos. His family compound was directly across from their hospital, and we were brought over to meet him and the governor of the state of Leyte.

Walking across the expansive lawn, through the guarded gates, we spotted three large helicopters. A lunch and business meeting was going on, and we were welcomed as honored guests. Philip, following lunch, offered his six-seater black EC-155 Eurocopter to view the devastation from the air. We were joined by the governor and his wife. Emotional and gut-wrenching, we viewed scenes you see in big-budget disaster films. When a 23-foot wave comes on shore and drags everything it can back out to sea, you are witness to Mother Nature's wrath. Huge cargo ships on their sides lay next to houses two miles inland. Giant oil tanks at the refinery, dented and twisted like toys from the air pressure differentials. And everywhere, for a 30-square-mile grid, homes without roofs, buildings crushed, coconut trees on their sides. We flew over the childhood compound of Imelda and her family, heavily damaged. The giant statue of Christ, looking over the people of Tacloban, still standing in its serene pose. Arms outstretched with palms up, I couldn't help but think that the statue itself was traumatized.

When we returned to the compound, Philip greeted us and walked us back to the hospital. He wanted to see the SunSpring in action. He also wanted the people of the town to be able to have free access to the safe water it produced. We began plans to run a pipe and multiple faucets out to the road.

Chaplain Blase, meanwhile, had been in contact with the town manager. He had requested that we place the second SunSpring at a new health center in an area outside of town called Suhi. In the chaos, no address or directions were given. That evening, back at the hospital, we had dinner consisting of small chickens with very little meat on the bones, and rice. We asked our group of about 50 other aid workers if anyone had heard of the Suhi Health Center. We went to sleep that night wondering what tomorrow would bring and if we would be able to find our next installation site. Exhausted and in a deep sleep, someone stole Jack's large tool bag and his iPad, both laying within a foot of his head. As the Sun rose, Jack realized what happened and we all went on a panicked search of the grounds. We stumbled upon the thief's lair, where he emptied the backpack, throwing it in a heap with other trash.

The hospital assigned us a bodyguard for the rest of our stay. Dressed in a turban, military fatigues and an ominous AK-47, our guard enjoyed his new position. He showed us the additional weaponry hidden in his clothing–knives, pistols, even a grenade. He joined us in the bed of the pickup truck as we followed a second truck carrying the large crate, searching for the elusive Suhi Health Center. We arrived at a new, yet damaged building with a blown-out sign. Indeed, we had arrived at the health center, but it had never been occupied. Scheduled to be opened, the impending typhoon scuttled plans. On the grounds surrounding the Center we saw piles of white bags. The smell was eye watering. Piles of dead bodies in zipped up white plastic bags were placed in what would have been a parking lot outside the health center. Jack and I were stunned and sickened by the odor in the hot Sun. This was referred to as the Mass Grave. As victims were recovered, they were brought to this abandoned field, out of the way.

I asked around why these bodies weren't claimed by family members. "Their families are also lying here," the Chaplain told us. "There is no one alive to claim them." *Seven hundred bodies by our estimate.* That turned out to be just 10% of the number of eventual victims to be recovered.

Back at the hospital, Reynaldo told us of his loss. His three older aunts were all drowned. Ruben, the hospital's maintenance chief, asked to walk us to the harbor. He wanted to show us something. The harbor was in ruins, with hundreds tending to the piers, to the wreckage. He brought us to a giant blue cargo hauler, listing and bobbing three quarters under the water. He stood in front, took a deep breath, and told me that it was at this boat that he lost his granddaughter. They were both dragged into the water when the wave came. "I held her tight. But she was ripped from my arms and disappeared under the hull of this blue boat," Reuben remembered. He wasn't even tearing up. I couldn't hold back my tears.

As we continued our walking tour of Hell, I noticed an oddity of disaster scenes, proven out many times since. One of the first commodities that arrives on scene is bottled water. Tons of it. Three weeks in, and the bottled water was becoming scarce. We would see big pockets of hoarders, but you can't blame them. Survival instincts trump community spirit. I also noticed dozens of water bladders the size of basketball courts distributed around the harbor district. With a huge Oxfam logo emblazoned on the material, and about 15 spigots connected, trucks fill these bladders with potable water. The problem is that they are using municipal water from the water treatment plant and adding large amounts of chlorine to kill the bacteria and other contaminants. I never saw a single person draw water from these bladders. I took a sip from one of the spigots, and it tasted and smelled like a swimming pool. Curious thing, even in desperation for drinking water, no one wants to drink chlorine. Good thing, because it's not healthy long term. Those 15 bladders had been partially refilled only once in the past three weeks.

Jack and I still had the second SunSpring on our agenda. We needed to find a place to install it. Surely, we weren't going to put it at the Mass Grave, and we didn't have a municipal water line available at the harbor. Chaplain Blase discovered that there were 1250 residents living across the road from the grave, about one mile inland. The residents of Suhi Barangay have only a single borehole for all the residents. Wide enough for a bucket, lowered by rope down 50 feet, filled with water and dragged back up. The only other source of water was across the street at the village infirmary. A 1000-liter tank sat empty. Once a week, a municipal water truck comes and fills it. The tank becomes empty just hours later.

We worked with the barefoot engineers and barangay captain to install the SunSpring in front of the infirmary, after sinking our submersible pump into the borehole. Residents worked with hand-made tools of nails and rocks to dig a channel in the asphalt road to accommodate the pump's tubing. Once completed, the town celebrated. Safe drinking water was available.

Since the typhoon, the barangay, as most other places on the island, sat in total darkness at night. With no electricity, the women of the community were more concerned about how this nightly grind was starting to affect the families. The next day, Jack and I returned to Cebu to return to the US. But first we stopped at a large hardware store, recently well stocked. I bought a large, overpriced generator and 12 street light fixtures and asked the Chaplain to deliver them to Suhi. Two days later, Chaplain Blase sent me photos from his phone. Christmas lights were strung, street lights were in place, and the community was partying for hours into the night.

Suhi, it turned out nine months later, became my biggest flop. I am embarrassed to say that the SunSpring sits idle today and has since 2014. The borehole dried up. This isn't surprising. Water tables shift around, and shallow holes into the Earth just don't guarantee endless extraction. We installed the SunSpring and broke our own rules. We were being first responders filling a need as best we could. In the chaos of the disaster, we put in an expensive piece of equipment without the benefit of a thoughtful process. A SunSpring is a fantastic water purification system. But it doesn't make water. Our first item, on a broad list of requirements, is to be sure there is an adequate raw water source. In the wet and the dry seasons. If we're pulling out of a well, we need a hydrologist's report to indicate that the recharge rate of the source is greater than the extraction rate of a SunSpring each day. Well, we didn't do any of that.

To make matters worse, I didn't have the time nor the peripheral vision to assess the political situation then or forecast into the future. On this, I can't beat myself up too much. The current leadership of the Philippines is a bit bonkers. Here's why that is relevant: There are over 40,000 barangays or barrios in the Philippines, each one headed by a barangay captain. Suhi's enthusiastic captain was a young man with plenty of energy and I worked well with him, despite the language barrier. When the borehole dried up months later, I reached out to every influential Filipino I knew—in the U.S. and on the islands. At three different Rotary International conventions since 2014, I had meetings with various Rotarians from the Philippines delegation and explained the problem. I told them that 1250 people in Suhi relied on a single borehole for years. It has dried out. There is a huge six-inch irrigation line moving across the valley just one mile from their road. We needed to tap into that line and recharge the borehole on a regular basis.

One after the other, I was promised an answer. If I had a dime for every time I heard the phrase "No problem," I would have a few bucks. Finally, at the Atlanta convention in 2017, I got a definitive answer from Marco, a Rotarian from Manila.

Marco: "You know why nothing is moving on the water issue for Suhi Barangay?"

Jon: "No, I'm dying to know. Keeps me up at night with guilt."

Marco: "There are drug dealers living in that barrio."

Jon: "But there are also women and children, and they need safe drinking water."

Marco: "I understand that. But the policy of President Dutarte is to starve out those barangays that harbor drug dealers."

Jon: "But it's been three years. When does the starving end?"

Marco: "It's more a policy of indifference. That can last forever."

And so it goes. H2OpenDoors and Rotary are poor first responders. When we can practice measured and thoughtful application of our philanthropic work, we are among the best 2nd and 3rd responders on the planet. Suhi will always provide a cautionary reminder to me that my heart must be linked to my brain at all times.

Rotary is perceived to be a first responder in many parts of the world, however. This is because on many tents that protect victims after earthquakes, hurricanes and typhoons, the Rotary logo is emblazoned on the fabric. From a news helicopter, this is very impressive. But Rotary just writes the checks to Shelter Box, a UK-based NGO who has partnered with Rotary International. Prepositioned for immediate deployment throughout the world, Shelter Boxes contain everything a family of six would need for a week or two: family tent, cook stove, meals, water safety gadget. The box costs $1000 and a donor can track his or her "adopted box" all over the planet from a cool app. Rotary is the largest donor to Shelter Box.

But it is the long, hard slog that Rotarians are best equipped to handle. Polio eradication is a gargantuan example. With mass immunizations by hundreds of thousands for tens of millions around the world, Rotary has brought us to the cusp of success. Like smallpox, polio is soon to be wiped off the face of the planet. Something like that requires an army of volunteers and millions of dollars. Rotary has stubbornly stuck to this mission for a couple of decades and roped in the Bill and Melinda Gates Foundation to ensure success.

PUERTO RICO, FEMA AND MATH

Ever since its inception in 1979, FEMA has been using bottled water as the very first response to disasters. Hundreds of millions of dollars for each disaster in pallets of cases of bottles. A C130 cargo transport plane can hold about 12 of these pallets, or about 20,400 half-liter bottles (around 5000 gallons). That tops out the maximum payload weight of 42,000 pounds.

What does FEMA pay for this bottled water? Their contract with Nestlé has them paying about 46 cents per gallon for the water. But when you factor in all of the transportation and logistics, that bottled water is costing the taxpayers $1.85 per gallon. A C130 load of 5000 gallons of purified bottled water therefore costs us $9,250 delivered to receiving points on scene. (By the way, one SunSpring purifies up to 5000 gallons every day for over 10 years, at an installed price of $25,000).

Now, stay with me here. One load of bottled water from FEMA for $9,250 will provide 5000 people with a gallon of water for a day. To provide a month's worth: $277,500 requiring *thirty C130 transports*. What were the total bottled water costs over 10 months of FEMA relief for the 3.3 million residents? My calculator doesn't go that high.

If you don't yet have blood running from your ears, listen to this: In September of 2018, one year after Hurricane Maria, photos and video footage on national news showed an entire runway with

20,000 *pallets* of bottled water just sitting there in the Sun. A stock-pile of over 38 *million single-use bottles* not distributed for months. With time and heat, the plastic leaches its chemical components into the water. If you've ever left a single-use bottle in your hot car for too long, you might notice it tastes a bit off. Well, that's why the stockpile just sat there. About 700 pallets had been distributed by the local Puerto Rican authorities, and they all had a very bad taste. A combination of plastic antimony and bacterial recontamination of the water contained within its walls might very well have contributed to massive illnesses the water distribution was intended to mitigate.

A month before the runway stockpile story broke, Darrell Ransom visited one of the SunSprings we installed in San Salvador Caguas. As FEMA Director for Distribution Management, Mr. Ransom has been dealing with the folly of bottled water disaster distributions for several years. He wants to change the game and use SunSprings instead. As I said, with an installed price of $25,000, the system will provide 5000 gallons every day for over 10 years. *That's a price of one tenth of a penny per gallon, compared to $1.85.* He was enthu-siastic about this approach, and we hope to soon see C130s filled with SunSprings deployed for rapid response. I'm rooting for the US Government to make the rational decision to end the lunacy of long term, mass distribution of bottled water. Let's all watch FEMA's decision-making for the next slate of disasters to see if they can kick the bottled water habit and get smart about this.

WHEN WILL WE GET OFF THE BOTTLE?

In 2017, bottled water became the most consumed beverage in North America, due in part to fears of lead-tainted water and con-cerns about the negative health effects of sugary beverages.

The 2016 Nestlé Annual Report shows $7.4 billion in sales from water alone. Nevertheless, the company pays nothing for the 150 gallons per minute it already pumps from the ground in central Michigan, or in several other US locations including Indian reservations and many hotspots around the globe. The king, Coca-Cola, increased sales of bottled water by 3.5%. Worldwide consumption is ever-increasing, as infrastructure costs rise at the same time consumer habits are solidifying. We trust the water in a sealed bottle in inverse proportion to international distrust of public sources. By the way, public drinking fountains are disappearing from every country faster than Blockbuster stores.

According to the most recent Statistica report for 2017, the largest per capita consumer country of bottled water might surprise you. United States? Nope. At a hefty 67 gallons per year per man, woman and child...Mexico. Number Two is Thailand, followed by Italy. Surprised by this? Well here's what is most shocking. The United States is Number Four, at 42 gallons per year per capita. Considering that the U.S. has the Clean Water Act, and that you have every alternative to bottled water, we still consume more than France, Germany, The UAE or Spain per person. We do so because we can. Numero Uno Mexico has few alternatives, and so bottled water is the primary method for safe hydration.

Yet, as mentioned previously in this book, the rural poor spend between 1/3 and 1/2 of their daily income on bottled water. So, many Mexicans choose the less expensive Coke to hydrate, not aware that sugary, caffeinated beverages actually dehydrate the body. Mexico has become the world's greatest medical tourism destination for kidney and gall stone removal. Many factors are responsible for the build-up of the stones in the first place, but when you don't drink enough water every day, the stones won't pass through your system, continuing to grow.

The staggering growth of the bottled water industry is the classic good and evil story. Getting safe drinking water to seven billion Earthlings is no small task. We've got to find alternatives to the fact that globally *one million single-use bottles are discarded every minute!* The H2OpenDoors project has always rejected the single-use bottle in favor of large, family-sized refillable containers, sanitized prior to filling. Plastic is not evil. Using plastic once and throwing it away after one use (because refilling can extend the useful life of a bottle increasing the potential for release of chemical toxins) *is madness.*

MARKETING JUGGERNAUTS

Brands are a fascination to me. Always have been. That's why I've co-owned a marketing firm for a few decades. One of the questions I always ask potential clients is: "*Why aren't there Honda Motorcycle Tattoos?*" Thought provoking, isn't it? Harley-Davidson has positioned its iconic logo and image so well, that devotees will permanently brand their arm, leg or neck with the HD trademark. I find this astounding. Even more amazing is that a large percentage of those with a Harley tattoo don't even ride the damn things and may not even ride any motorcycle at all. *What have they done in Milwaukee that Honda hasn't?* What do companies have to learn from this rabid affection, almost religious affiliation with a motorcycle manufacturer? How does a loyal, self-described Harley guy or gal align their self-image and value set with the imagery that Harley and its ad agencies have honed over the last 100 years?

But nothing has made the marketing history Hall of Fame faster and bigger that the rise of bottled water. The very first PET (polyethylene terephthalate) single use, disposable bottle was introduced by Coca-Cola for sodas in 1978. It was an immediate hit. Lighter than previous plastics and glass (yes, I am old enough to remember soda in glass bottles), the PET bottle was innovation with a capital I.

The 1967 film, *The Graduate*, starring Dustin Hoffman, had a scene that continues to resonate to this day:

Mr. McGuire: *I want to say one word to you. Just one word.*

Benjamin: *Yes, sir.*

Mr. McGuire: *Are you listening?*

Benjamin: *Yes, I am.*

Mr. McGuire: *Plastics.*

Benjamin: *Exactly how do you mean?*

Mr. McGuire: *There's a great future in plastics. Think about it. Will you think about it?*

Fast-forward to 2017, and bottled water had overtaken all other beverages in the U.S. at 13.7 billion gallons, according to the International Bottled Water Association. The first bottled water brand I remember as a young man was Perrier. With its sophisticated, foo-foo image and marketing, it was a perfect complement to that mustard commercial with the guy leaning out of his Rolls-Royce to ask the other rich dude if he had any Grey Poupon. The next big brand was Evian. As Robin Williams pointed out, "Did you ever wonder that Evian is Naive spelled backwards?"

But my water brand Lifetime Achievement Award has got to go to Fiji Waters. Owned since 2004 by the billionaire odd couple, Stewart and Lynda Resnick, they built their fortune with Teleflora. When they bought their first orange groves in Kern County, California, Lex Luther-like business deals catapulted them to fame in the late 80s, buying farms on the cheap in the drought years. They soon became the largest producers of almonds, pistachios and pomegranates in the world. You know their brands: POM Wonderful, Halo Clementines, Wonderful Pistachios and Almonds and more. The Resnick's secret to success had to do with, wait for it...water. You see, they owned the biggest share of the Kern Water Bank. In previous decades, the

State of California had spent over $75 million to develop a massive, underground aquifer, and then mysteriously transferred ownership to some Kern County officials. These guys then gave almost all of it over to Westside Mutual Water Company. Westside was a private water supplier, owned by, you guessed it, the Resnicks.

If this all sounds sleazy to you, a superior court judge agreed in 2014. The court cases are still going on. But in the meantime, the Resnicks consume more water *just for their citrus farms* than the entire City of San Francisco. Pistachios and almonds from California are the favorites of the Chinese, who don't care that to grow one almond requires five gallons of water. Like *Chinatown*, the film from the 70s starring Jack Nicholson, water barons are enormously powerful in California, with dozens of in-house attorneys working through a maze of claims and counter-claims.

Ten years before their legal troubles, back in 2004, the Resnicks heard that Canadian billionaire David Gilmore was looking to sell the company he founded in 1996 on Fiji Island. They snapped up Fiji Water for $50 million. It was an easy decision, since the Fijian government was only charging a tax of one-third of a Fijian cent per liter to pull from an aquifer. The factory was built directly over the aquifer, allowing the claim "never touched by human hands" to become the tagline on the colorful label. The iconic square PET bottle, produced and shipped from China at an amazingly low price, combined with the romance of a natural aquifer in Fiji made the product the island nation's number one export. The Resnicks' cost on a liter bottle, all in, was around 45 cents, landed in the Port of San Francisco. It sold at wholesale for $1.25 and retail for over $2. Great business.

Before long, political turmoil festered in Fiji and the military took over, raising that tax from one third cent to 15 cents per liter. The Resnicks responded in typical flair and bellicose. They shut down the factory and fired all the workers. That lasted one day. The government threatened to seize the factory and the water rights.

Stanley and Lynda reluctantly paid the higher tax, and Fiji continues to flourish as the brand we scratch our heads about. Why do we need this water in the United States? The carbon expenditures to move the bottles to Fiji from China, then to ship the filled bottles across the Pacific are enormous. For what? The water is fine, sure. But we can purify water here and put it in bottles. Doesn't matter. Some people like their Harley tattoos, and others gotta have that square bottle with the pretty label. Marketing is pretty powerful.

In a bold marketing campaign, the Resnicks unleashed their ad agency to get aggressive, pitting Fiji bottled water against city tap water. The 2006 full-page ad campaign showed the bottle and blared, "The label says Fiji because it's not bottled in Cleveland." This was not received well in Cleveland as you might expect. The public utilities director, Julius Ciaccia, decided to get the Fiji water tested. The lab results showed 6.31 micrograms of arsenic per liter. Big backfire! Fiji promptly recalled the campaign. People still buy that water, but I avoid it for now a new reason: *arsenic is not good for you!*

Ethically, Fiji Water has more problems than a massive carbon footprint. The local Fijians aren't allowed access to this aquifer. With over 50 million gallons of water being extracted each year and traveling to the well-heeled in far-away lands, the people that live on the island face continued water scarcity. Recently, there has been scrambling efforts for rain harvesting that are quite remarkable, in their own right. However, what happens in the dry season? And can rain be the water source for just under one million Fijians? Math is more powerful than marketing.

Agricultural water math is even more amazing in the United States. Farmers buy their irrigation water by the acre-foot from water boards in California for an average of $70. That's 326,000 gallons for just $70. That same raw water, run through a purification system and bottled, has a value of $2.4 million. With raw resources so cheap, why should farmers conserve? If gasoline was to cost 10 cents a gallon, there wouldn't be a reason for fuel effi-ciency standards. But there are larger things at play than the laws of supply and demand, and "what the market will bear." Things like the health of our Earth, sustainability and availability of a limited set of resources for all mankind.

Water and agriculture barons like the Resnicks are capitalists. I don't fault them for that. But we don't need to revert to socialism to figure out how to get out of the bind we are facing. Agriculture is responsible for over 75% of all fresh water withdrawals around the globe. In some regions of the world, it's more like 90%. Very little is returned to the watershed. We're expected to have another 2.5 billion people on the planet by 2050. Where is the innovation and leadership? A moonshot project for the next decade ought to focus on *how to make agriculture use half as much water.* Universities and industry should be given every incentive possible to tackle this and invent solutions.

In a small but effective way, Jack Barker's patented invention of the SunSpring contributes to a solution. The recycling and cleaning up of water sources for human consumption is laudable in its own right. But Jack is also demonstrating that higher yields and greater efficiency is realized when ag uses treated water. Growers can see a 25% increase in yield. Optimized crop protection, targeted drip irrigation and the increase of a crop's drought tolerance all contribute to solutions. One apple requires 70 liters of water to be produced. That's more than the amount of water an adult should drink in a full month.

Irrigated farm land has doubled over the past 50 years. We are running out of time. The lion's share of water use is from the agri-culture industry in the United States. So, the good news is that we have a bit of control on our own territory to demand sanity in water use. We did an effective job of legislating higher efficiencies in fuel usage from the automotive industry back in 1973. Congress established Corporate Average Fuel Economy (CAFE), mostly in response to the big oil embargo of the same year. Cars manufactured after 1978 required the new car fleet to average 27.5 mpg by the year 1985. Done in phases, we have gotten to an enviable point now where we will see a 49.6% mpg average by 2025, with electric cars leading the surge. We would never have gotten to this point without congressional action starting it off.

Same holds true for our water conundrum. Agriculture is using 85% of the fresh water. Congress could legislate a 15% reduction in ag's use of water by, say, 2025. The methods to increase efficiencies are largely developed, and universities can continue the research. *The only thing lacking is leadership.* We all need to get on the bandwagon. Whatever innovations we can use to solve our problem can be exported to solve water scarcity around the globe.

THE FALLACY OF
THE NONPROFIT

The name "nonprofit" is the other n-word that I disdain. Why is organizational categorization based on what is or what isn't left over after all the money has been spent? Who coined this term?

"Not-for-Profit" isn't much better. I'm old enough to remember when the dominant term was "charity." I might hate that one even more.

It's frustrating to me, as I own and manage a "for-profit" company with employees, and I also direct and manage the affairs of a "nonprofit" charitable project with volunteers. The way I prefer to separate the descriptions, however, is that my marketing firm is an enterprise, and my passion project is "service above self," using Rotary parlance. Problem with that, of course, is the former sounds permanent while the latter smacks of benevolent, yet temporary impulses.

A wise man said, "It's all done with words." Whatever we call it, intent is important. The moniker "nonprofit" connotes that the intent of the work of a nonprofit is to not make profit. Weird. Adam Braun started what he calls a "For-Purpose" organization. Pencils for Purpose has built over 200 schools so far, and his book, *The Promise of a Pencil*, describes his journey. That feels a bit better.

Rotary refers to itself as an "international service organization" made up of over a million volunteers, grouped in 35,000 little tribes around the globe. The Rotary Foundation is a 501(c)(3) organization that is monitored by watchdogs like Charity Navigator. With a consistent four-star rating every year, the governance and frugality is some of the best in the world. That's why I wanted to do my work and expand my vision within an organization like that. Rotary, in collaboration with the Bill and Melinda Gates Foundation are very close to eradicating polio off the face of the Earth. Hundreds of millions of dollars have been directed to this goal, with immunizations as the primary strategy. Much like the successful eradication of smallpox after thousands of years, polio has been a stubborn foe, now close to extinction.

If anyone asks me how to start doing good works with real social impact–and they don't often–I would advise them to avoid starting their own charitable organization. The sad fact is that if I had started H2OpenDoors as a nonprofit charitable organization on its own, and I was going to operate it full time in the early, formidable years, I would be a one-star organization at best. Necessarily, I would need to pay my mortgage, feed my family, buy gas or electricity for my car. I would need to scrape 10-20% off of every contributed dollar for my own survival. Then, because I wouldn't have any support system, I would need to pay for administrative help and pay for promotion to get noticed. Conservatively, less than half of the money I would raise would go to the beneficiaries I intended to help. Sadly, there are far too many small charitable groups that operate in this manner, with the smallest part of their revenue pie going to the actual work they are chartered to perform.

So, I choose to operate the project without salaries or administrative expenses. A solid cadre of volunteers, technicians and consultants have surrounded me since the beginning. As a project of the larger social impact ecosystem of Rotary, H2OpenDoors can take every single dollar of contributions and apply it to the equipment and tools needed to provide clean water or innovative educational systems. With excited volunteers and a grant system that can even match any monies raised, I was able to get productive from Day One.

My advice is to plug into a larger power pack. Take advantage of their name and reputation. Transparency and oversight in multiple ways are hallmarks of the best of these organizations. You don't hear about scandals or misappropriation of funds at Rotary because there aren't any. For over a century, Rotary has been a part of Americana to be exported proudly.

There are other large service organizations that do wonderful work as well. Kiwanis, Lions, Optimists. Solid and dependable, many of these are finally shaking the "old white guy" image. They are becoming diverse, with larger and larger percentages of women, people of color, and younger enthusiasts.

Because I walk on two slippery banana peels in the "enterprise" and "service" worlds, I attend a lot of conventions. There's always a slate of keynote speakers, breakout sessions and a trade show floor. When you're at a Rotary International Convention, held in a different country every June, you'll join at least 30,000 other Rotarians from all over the world. But five minutes into your visit to the booths in a Rotary trade show, called the House of Friendship, you notice something very, very different. Every exhibit is a different project. Proudly represented by a Rotary volunteer, often the woman or man that dreamed up the initiative, they will show how it works and offer to collaborate with you. No sales are happening. Think huge science fair. Or service fair. With implemented solutions from agricultural initiatives boosted by microfinance, to wheelchair projects assembled in local communities, to innovative water provisioning and healthcare solutions, you will get chills as you walk up and down the aisles. With over 1000 exhibits, you will get a sense that there isn't a problem that can't be tackled by people who really care. You will be uplifted. You won't have any time, anymore, to be critical and frustrated with the slow pace of change. Inspiration works like that. It replaces cynicism with your own flashes of genius to make an immediate difference.

The 2017 Rotary International Convention was held in Atlanta at the World Congress Center at Olympic Park. The center is next door to the headquarters of CNN. During the three days of the convention, there was perpetual coverage about Trump, Russians, Collusion. That was all. Not a single reporter or cameraman walked a few dozen feet to come into the House of Friendship and view and report on solutions that really matter–hundreds of them. Each one with the potential to save lives, elevate the poor, break perpetual cycles of poverty. Why wasn't it covered? *Where are our priorities as a species?*

VOLUNTOURISM AS A THING

When any of us go on vacation, it takes us a couple of days to unwind. But when you go to where I go with my merry band of water warriors, it's different. There isn't internet coverage and very weak cellular. You immediately give up on even trying to launch your smartphone. The first thing I notice within an hour of arriving in the region is the relief of neck tension I had been so used to.

Back home, we all tend to walk through the streets of our towns with our heads down, intent on answering that email or text message. FOMO (Fear of Missing Out) has us tethered to our devices 15 hours a day. Might as well have a kettle bell necklace.

But when you're in a region without cell service, you immediately look up and out. You become excited and intrigued about what might be on the horizon or around the next bend of the road. You are stimulated by the strangeness. You are profoundly moved at every new encounter you have and each new connection you make. I've always felt that I find my true self, how I was designed to be, when I'm in these communities.

We've been curating unique experiences ever since we started to bring people with us to help provide service. Our time is usually an 80/20 mix, with the smaller amount devoted to service, and the bulk of our time becoming immersed in the community and the culture, doing some wicked fun adventure as well. I used to feel guilty about that. Thank you, Jewish Mom. I am over that.

Installing a SunSpring is a five to six-hour task if we have four experienced people on that crew. If we have more people, it takes longer. We usually split up into project teams: four on the SunSpring, and everyone else doing projects set up by the nearby school or the women of the village. Gardening projects, painting, anything that can be accomplished in one day, working alongside the kids and families of the village. Usually by about 4PM, we're all done, and the village has prepared a feast or dance presentation and other ways to honor our gift and welcome us like visiting dignitaries.

We stay an extra day amongst our new friends. This is when we train a small village technical crew on the monthly maintenance procedures and discuss the ways they can launch a water sales enterprise. On some expeditions, we've also prearranged to install and train with the RACHEL educational system for their school, provided there are at least 250 students in the area.

Once our two days of service is complete, we are on the move. We never install a SunSpring in an area without also surveying another site for a future installation or two. And we often take some time out to get a geo-political perspective from a respected leader in that country. For Mexico, that has always been Vicente Fox.

For all five of our Mexican installations, we've spent a couple days at Centro Fox. Part presidential library, part international conference center, we get to wind down in palatial sleeping quarters and luxurious surroundings of their family hacienda-turned hotel. President Fox has always been gracious with his time, spending a couple hours at lunch and then a private meet and greet. When we have brought along high school students, the Centro Fox staff conducts a President of the Day exercise. A "president" is elected by the group, a cabinet is formed, and everyone gathers around the desk that President Fox used when he served from 2000-2006. Issues are discussed and participants are challenged by fashioning referendums and statements.

During one Q&A, one of our high school students, Andrew, asked President Fox a question, "You served for six years. Were you able to accomplish everything you wanted to?" Fox smiled and said, "Let me put it to you this way. In the United States, you have two parties, and roadblocks at every turn. In Mexico, we have 21 parties. So, no. I didn't get through my agenda. That's why I'm still working!"

We always wrap things up with a two or three-day adventure. In Nepal, 18 hearty souls went on a three-day trek through the Annapurna range of the Himalayas. The fact that I survived it is a rare, proud memory. In Kenya, we were hosted by Maasai warriors and stayed in basecamps. Morning and afternoon game drives took us out on the search for the Big Five, seen within hours at the beginning of the Great Migration in the Mara. In Nicaragua, four great bubbling volcanos with fascinating guided tours. Future trips to Peru will include Machu Picchu and Ecuador will include a few days on the Galapagos Islands.

Our expedition to India is in the planning stages at this writing. The 30 people registered for this 12-day voluntourism experience will participate in two days of polio immunizations near Agra on Polio Mega Days in January 2019. Over one million children will be immunized throughout the country during that campaign. The partnership of Rotary International and the Gates Foundation is a large reason why polio is so very close to complete eradication. Then, we'll travel 30km to install a SunSpring water bottling plant in a large village, anxious to start a water enterprise. By the way, polio is a waterborne disease. We'll also put in a RACHEL system at the Rotary school of 800 children. Our final four days will include a behind-the-ropes tour to the major sites of Northern India, and some of us will extend to go down to Ranthambore National Park to view Bengal tigers and elephants in the wild.

THE GOOD, THE BAD AND THE UGLY

Voluntourism, like microfinance, are terms that get used inappropriately at times. The first practitioners were visionaries, using disruptive strategies and tactics to improve and inspire world travel in the former, and empowerment of the poor in the latter. I was at a Rotary International conference where one of the keynote speakers was Muhammad Yunus, the Nobel Prize-winning founder of Grameen Bank and of microfinance. The Banker to the Poor, as he has become known, was particularly concerned at the time. Since his award and multiple magazine covers, the term "microfinance" was being misused to brand a plethora of financial instruments. Not only was this tainting the original notion, it was being done so in pursuit of profit, none of which was benefitting the poor.

Voluntourism, in its purest form, stems from desire to serve. A growing number of young workers in Silicon Valley or IT Lagoon don't want to travel like our parents did. They're less interested in the cruise and caviar experiences, and more interested in the village experience. They want to leave a mark. They want to serve, and then connect with the locals, and then have fun. For our Africa expeditions, I often bill it as Service, Soul, Safari.

However, ask someone like JK Rowling, the author extraordinaire of Harry Potter and more, and you'll get a rolled-up nose when you talk about voluntourism. Ms. Rowling and others have been quite vocal about the negatives. It's a shame, because done in the right way, profound connections and permanent improvements can impact and benefit a community for years. Lumos, the charity Ms. Rowling founded, works to expose exploitive practices and orphanages that use them. Rowling said some institutions use voluntourism to gouge money from wealthy travelers to care for children, who could be abused, starved or even trafficked. "There are children that are being severely abused and neglected, but children tell us that they are told they have to smile and sing and tell the volunteers they love them, otherwise they'll be beaten or locked up or they won't get food," she said.

I don't know who coined the term, but I first heard it back in 2005. Volunteer tourism is popular, which has attracted some unscrupulous operators who simply do it to make a buck. The brochure shows vacation scenes and makes vague reference to the service work. As with any activity, you should do some good old-fashioned vetting. There are dishonest players out there.

Volunteers might also take paying jobs from locals in need of money. This was one effect after volunteering spiked in Haiti after the earthquake in 2010. With only volunteers and no tourism and a lack of work, many were homeless with no income to improve the situation. Some non-government organizations (NGOs) and tour operators charge fees for the privilege of volunteering on their "missions." Certain crucial questions should always be asked when considering support or participation in any project or nonprofit organization:

1. What percent of these fees go to the service project, and what percentage goes to staff, overhead and promotion?
2. Do you have verified case studies, videos and interviews on the actual service work they've accomplished?
3. Most importantly, can I speak to at least two past participants?

If they can't or won't provide answers that satisfy these basic questions, then simply bow out of your support. An H2OpenDoors project is, by its very nature, a philanthropic endeavor. Rotary projects always are. There is no paid staff, and every dime spent to go on an expedition or work brigade goes towards funding the actual equipment to be deployed, the accommodations and food and ground transportation needs. We pay for our own travel to these countries. We make a video with interviews after these trips and return one year later for follow up. Our partner Rotary clubs or participating NGOs in the region give us continuous feedback as to the efficacy and sustainability we are most focused on. And since most of our participants come to us from word of mouth from previous travelers, there aren't any surprises, only amazement at the impact our small contributions make on thousands of people.

The mandate for us is that we must leave behind a permanent solution to their most pressing challenge: the access to safe, drinking water. But we also view our mission as using technology to unlock the human potential of the village and the school. Together with businessmen in the nearby region through their Rotary involvement, we provide *mentorship* on how to start and run a business, *monitoring* and oversight on the care and feeding of the equipment and *microfinance* to provide the incidental funding to run the enterprise. I call it the 3Ms.

After one year, we expect that the small social business has sprouted wings and is generating real profit to be used, exclusively, for the essential social services of the community. Things like providing protein in meals at school, building proper latrines, classroom expansion, laptops for the computer lab, or a RACHEL educational system for Grades 3 through 12. This is a big, fat list of real benefits.

The village and its people aren't props for our Facebook posts. They are evidence of significant work, having the potential to change the trajectory of lives *towards self-reliance*. When we return the following year, these same people show their gratitude and affection in authentic ways. We don't continually give and give. If we've done our jobs correctly in Year One, we can let them treat us to a nice meal and a dance presentation in Year Two. In the best circumstances, they are earning revenue to provide for their most basic needs. We offer guidance for good governance, and our affection for many years going forward.

My personal favorite emails and photos to receive from these places are from new friends I've met, wearing a robe from their college graduations, or holding their new baby. I feel that I've got hundreds of new neighbors. My neighborhood stretches across oceans.

Ms. Rowling and others have a point of view and sense of cynicism with good reason. But, as the proverbial baby and the bath water, be discerning in your criticism. There is Voluntourism, and then there is "small v" voluntourism. Microfinance and microfinance.

MY FAVORITE DOPAMINE SURGES

There are several of the same touch points in every installation that bring me profound satisfaction. The first one is visual. As we arrive at the site, and we walk towards the concrete slab we asked the village to create a month before, we see the unopened, 1,000-pound crate sitting next to it. To make that scene possible required months of planning, and in many cases, a fair share of anxiety.

Funding of about $28,000 had to be acquired. A site survey had to have been performed, and a proper water lab analysis completed and reviewed. Capacity analysis needed to be done to satisfy that raw water will be available all 365 days a year and that the source can recharge to allow for extractions of 5000 gallons a day. Specific instructions on the creation of a reinforced concrete slab had to be provided to the village engineer, and the pouring of the slab had to be accomplished a month before our arrival in order to allow for sufficient curing. The SunSpring, with the appropriate configuration for the particular water conditions, had to be ordered from the factory, crated for international shipment and cleared through customs with at least two weeks cushion. We would have already scheduled and promoted the expedition. With up to 25 people joining us on the adventure, a hiccup with any of these moving parts can trip up our timetable. More than once, we've arrived in-country to learn that the crate was still at the airport's customs warehouse.

Executing a complex series of transactions and communications with people you know and understand is hard enough. Now try this with a brand-new set of characters, who you've never done this with before. In some cases, you are using Google Translate to guide your work. You're responsible for pushing each process through, encouraging your counterparts to treat these steps with as high a priority as you do. They invariably start with much bravado and arrogance. And as situations unwind and our arrival date draws closer, your foreign partners gain some humility. The pre-installation stages and mission-critical dates are not for the faint of heart. I tend to live on Pepto-Bismol for a full month before I'm on the plane to our village.

But then you walk up to the site, and you let out a big exhalation. Four months of preparation pay off big in dopamine surges to your brain. The hard work is behind you. Now you get members of the village to help you open up the crate, and the fun begins. My friends Brad Harris, Alex Buck, Liz Baun and Mary Jo Bagger especially love this part. They actually traveled to the factory in Colorado to learn how to install the SunSprings. Soulful people, they are a blast to travel the world with. Along with my girlfriend, Michelle Nirenstein, we enjoy skipping down the yellow brick roads of Nicaragua, Nepal, Kenya...you name it. The opening of the crate needs a soundtrack and theme song. Note to self: contact John Williams.

Because the SunSpring is cylindrical, and the crate is cubic, we need to stuff the void with material. In our earliest installs, we had a large donation of surplus Croc shoes. These are the weird and colorful shoes made famous by Mario Battali, before he creeped us all out. They turn out to be the perfect shoe for the developing world. Antimicrobial, they don't smell and are fully washable. We would stuff the crate with hundreds of pairs for kids and adults alike. When the lid is first opened, we begin distributing the gifts to the village elders. In a couple Northern Thailand hill tribes, we had shoes for just about every age, in every color of the rainbow. The Crocs donations dried up. Perhaps because I was dating the co-founder of the company at the time, and then I wasn't. We switched it up to flat soccer balls and hand pumps. Different commodity, same happy result.

Once the Cracker Jack surprises are removed from the crate, we need six people to help us roll out the big, diamond-plated can, carry it to the middle of the concrete slab, and raise it to rest on its base. Then, we drill multiple holes into the concrete and secure the can with expanding concrete bolts. All the components are pre-installed by the factory, except for the heavy batteries, pump, solar panels, wind turbine, and giant mast to hold them. Configuring a SunSpring in the field is easy. We usually have it up and processing purified water within four hours. As we go, we're training three or four village technicians that have been assigned to the project.

We often call them Barefoot Engineers. They rarely have a technical education in the formal sense. But every village has a cluster of men, and an occasional woman, who can fix anything. The solution they devise might not be elegant, but it is often genius. In the middle of a cornfield in the earthquake region of Nepal, I needed a ladder. Within 30 minutes, one of the guys created a strong bamboo ladder to the perfect specifications I needed. Another one welded a drill bit to the chuck of a 30-year-old electric drill, connected 200 feet of wire to a transformer, saving the day when our Ryobi 24V cordless drill broke. Recently, on Lamu, we ran out of PVC elbows to make a turn of pipe. One of the village techs, Mustafa, fashioned a kiln out of coral rocks. Once it was hot enough, he inserted a long, straight length of PVC and gently bent it to a perfect 90-degree angle. What these MacGyvers learn by doing should be written down in a textbook for every engineering school in the United States. I am constantly impressed and inspired by their knowledge, hard-earned.

The next emotional payoff is the ceremony for the "first drink." I usually have that honor and responsibility. I am a taste freak. The purified water that comes out of the SunSpring is 99.999% pathogen-free. I'm never worried that what was in the water before is still there. The membrane strands, 25,000 of them, have isolated all the bacteria, cysts and viruses, and the system flushes these out safely several times a day. The pure water has been forced under pressure through microscopic pores in the membranes' sides and out through the top and bottom of the strands. Picture angel-hair pasta that is hollow. This is ultrafiltration (UF), and the process is used every day in larger scale at water treatment plants throughout the world. Reverse-osmosis, or RO, is a similar process, but with much smaller pores. The water waste is around 60%, but with these UF systems, water waste is only 3%.

We use UF membrane technology because we want to retain the essential minerals in the water. Look at any store-bought water and you'll see that bottlers most likely use RO, and then add essential minerals back in, for taste and for health. Elements like sodium, calcium, potassium and magnesium. We need these electrolytes and minerals in our bodies and in our drinking water. Sometimes there are dissolved components in the water that can pass through the pores of an ultrafiltration membrane. We would have seen if any of these are pathogenic from the lab report, and if so, we would have added the appropriate media to mitigate that issue in the configuration at the factory. In some locations, heavy metals like arsenic and fluoride are starting to show up in water pulled out of deeply-drilled boreholes. We can treat those, as well, in the configuration at the factory.

Sometimes there is just a taste to the clean water that reflects a bit of the primary minerals. The community has always tasted it before, because they were drinking it when it also contained bacterial and viral contaminants. *But I want to make the water taste crisp.* We usually finish the water off with a Granular Activated Charcoal (GAC) housing that we hook inline if we have any taste or odor issues. This always does the trick. I then conduct a blind taste test between the new SunSpring water and the bottled water bought from a store. When no difference can be detected by 20 or more from the village and our team, we declare the SunSpring open for business for at least the next 10 years. Festivities commence, cigars are lit and the village executive presents us with a cup of their finest moonshine.

But this doesn't complete the dopamine payoff for all of our months in preparation. The Sally Field Academy Award moment where we can say, "*You love me, you really love me,*" happens when children and their mothers begin to line up for their bottles and walk off to their huts and home sites. They are smiling and clearly happy. A major stress has been lifted. The gathering of water, the long hikes to the water points, the bouts with diarrhea and stomach pain, the wasteful need to boil the water... these are, forever more, alleviated stress points. We take it for granted. They do not.

"For me, the greatest highlight on an H2OpenDoors expedition was in 2017 when we completed the installation at Nhobola village in Tanzania," Brad remembered. "The Chinese pump had failed to move the well water to the tank, and dozens of village women and children lined up at the well with buckets and jerry cans to lower with rope in order to capture this raw and contaminated water." It turned out that the well had a small mountain of silt building up, which in turn clogged up the pump. We worked with the barefoot engineers to dig out the silt, remove the frogs and restore the pump. Meanwhile, the SunSpring installation was almost complete.

"The first turn of the spigot that filled a sanitized bottle was, for me, deeply moving and profound," Brad said. "As Jon likes to say, you can leverage amazing change with just a little bit of technology and a whole lot of soul."

Our RACHEL team took a few photos while I was off with the water team in Tanzania. The intense engagement by three of the teachers of Busiya's secondary school was just beautiful. They became excited to learn a new way to teach, to get out of the way a bit and facilitate learning. "This is a brand-new concept, but with the right tools, most teachers would prefer this methodology over the boring, linear recitations and assignments," Michelle reported after the session. Students learn at different paces, but if you can help spark excitement and curiosity...well, you've hit the jackpot in education. We will continue to include this aspect in all our work at villages and schools going forward. We've now got a core group to begin to establish the RACHEL systems anywhere we go. And it's in perfect alignment with our overall mission of Water, Education, Peace.

GRINGO EPIPHANIES

We've done five installations in Mexico in the past few years. I enjoy working in Mexico for a few reasons. First, it's closer, so it's cheap and fast travel when compared to the other places around the world we commit to. Second, as previously mentioned, we have a warm friendship with Vicente and Marta Fox. Their support and hospitality is without equal. Third, I like to demonstrate to my fellow Americans that it is better to build bridges than walls.

All the expeditions give witness to personal transformations and insights gained among friends that have participated. They see travel in a new way, gaining access to perspectives not offered to the typical traveler or described in a guide book. This was especially profound for several people on one of our projects in Mexico a couple years ago. Alice and Jerry Rost are very old friends of mine for over 40 years. They brought their 14-year-old grandson, Zachary. I was thrilled, because Mexico has been a great place to bring students, albeit not without risks. We always have a stealthy security team, as we are generally in a couple of large vans moving about the country. We never travel at night. If you employ some common sense and reasonable precautions, you can relax into the culture and warmth that still thrives south of our border.

Recently I brought 20 high school students down for one week, and we spent two full days at Centro Fox following a SunSpring installation. During a "President For the Day" exercise conducted by the staff, mentioned earlier, one of the students is elected by the others to become President of Mexico. They get to wear the presidential sash, sit behind Fox's desk that is in a replicated office from his official Mexico City days, and conduct a meeting with his or her cabinet. Issues of the day are discussed as to how Mexico should respond to various international matters, and then they drill down to what teenagers would be interested in. Usually, topics like music, dating, social media and whether weed should be legalized.

Perhaps because he was the youngest and felt the most out of place, Zachary "won" the presidency. The little wallflower became the despot. I don't think we all laughed so hard in our lives. Zachary had been raised a bit entitled and a little spoiled in San Diego. Two 19 year-olds on the trip with us, Zack and Austin, straightened him out in a hurry. Not appreciating the eye-rolling, one-word responses he was giving his grandmother, they tag-teamed him. "Hey, dude. Show your grandmother some respect," Zach cautioned. "If you want to hang out with us, you've got to be a lot cooler," Austin pitched in. "Cool means respecting your betters." Little Zachary, wide-eyed and humbled, nodded his head in compliance. For the rest of the trip, Alice was provided with a pillow for her back, a daily cup of coffee, and frequent hugs from her grandson.

Austin and Zack are sons of two of my oldest friends. Glen Stoner and Warren Katz live in the New York area, and I've known them both for decades. I met Warren when we were as young as their sons were on that trip. I felt so honored that these guys entrusted me with their boys on this adventure. I could see similar personalities seeping out of their younger selves, and it was a bit surreal and very wonderful. When we arrived at Casa Alfan, an orphanage near Leon, Mexico where we often visit, Zach and Austin were rock stars.

Casa Alfan houses 60 Mexican orphans, aged 5-17, usually dropped there by a working mother who has escaped from an abusive alcoholic husband. The mothers have a really rough road ahead, often taking on three jobs, with no ability to raise the kids. Prior to spending an afternoon at Casa Alfan, we first go to the giant Costco located in Leon for "Supermarket Sweep." This game is comprised of three teams, three shopping carts, and 20 minutes. My instructions involve telling the players to load their baskets with necessities for the shelter. We aren't looking for candy or Twinkies. We want nutritious food and useful items. When I say "go," the three teams fan out.

In this edition, Zack Katz's team rolled to the checkout lane first and explained why they chose what was in their basket. The steaks and chicken were for five separate meals for the 60 kids because they had the highest protein. The six soccer balls because they assumed there was probably one ball for all the kids. The flats of eggs and boxes of fruit and vegetables rounded out the haul. The other teams did just as well but weren't as fast. We loaded up the bounty into our van and headed out to the orphanage.

The Alfan kids always help us unload into the refrigerators, and the staff points and directs. When Zack and Austin carried in the soccer balls, the younger kids began climbing on them trying to snatch them away. These young men showed me something about their character that day. Instead of brushing the horde of five-year-olds off as a nuisance, they turned it into a slow-motion wrestling match. Tossing children between them, these six-footers had kids up in the air, balanced on their shoulders, twisted under arms. It was like watching a Cirque du Soleil act. The kids–all 60 of them–were watching, laughing and shouting with glee. In five minutes, the ice was broken, and you would have thought the room was filled with cousins at Thanksgiving.

Following our SunSpring installation in the nearby community of Comonfort, we all drove to San Miguel de Allende. SMA is a gorgeous colonial-era town preserved in spice colors, with a wonderful music and art scene. Americans are drawn there, and a couple California friends of mine flourish as if they've lived there all their lives. President Fox's charitable organization had recently taken over a center for children with brain disorders called CRISMA. An innovative set of strategies to stimulate the brains of kids as young as one year, CRISMA receives families from all over Mexico. Mothers and their children sometimes travel by bus for two days to spend time under the care of a team of physical therapists, sound specialists and brain experts.

One of the members of the expedition, Jake Burke, was from Rhode Island. He had won a place on our Mexico expedition from a social media contest with a partner of ours, Causely, and their marketing channel called Sweat Angels. The channel is made up of over 3000 fitness business subscribers who encourage gym check-ins on Facebook and Instagram, thereby gaining exponential visibility for their facilities on those platforms. The cause of the month for July is always water and H2OpenDoors is the beneficiary. For every check-in, Causely sends us 20 cents, which amounts to about a $35,000 contribution each year.

Jake owns a couple large gymnasiums and a martial arts school. Large and muscular, he looks like a heavyweight boxer with a hard-earned belt. He has a heart of gold and, I learned, was orphaned as a boy. He connected with the kids at Casa Alfan, but his experience at CRISMA was most profound for him. "I look across the room, and there is this little boy with red-framed glasses and a big smile with a full set of braces on his teeth," Jake explained. "He was probably four or five, and his parents were killed in a car accident a year before, with the boy mangled in his car seat, jaw broken." Jake and the boy seemed to have their eyes locked on each other, with the broadest of smiles. As Jake tells the story to me after our visit, he is weeping. This brute of a man brought to a cascade of complex tears. Jake asked me if he could join Rotary in Rhode Island. He doesn't have to ask me or anyone, of course. But I encouraged him to pay that day forward. Find those things at home and internationally that motivate you, move you, and inspire others.

Such are the epiphanies and insights people get on these projects. We try to pack a lot into the trips besides a water system installation in the hopes that everyone finds the one "Jake moment," or the Zach and Austin experience, or the Alice in Grandson turnaround. I like to think of an H2OpenDoors expedition as a kind of Pee Wee Big Adventure where everyone has an opportunity to tap into the kind of soulful service that turns on their hearts. It might be water or education or disease prevention, or agriculture or community structures or microfinance, or any number of things that ring your own unique bell. That's the fun of it, and you'll never forget those moments—not ever.

BEST DAY OF MY LIFE

Two of our Mexico installations were made possible by the most delightful confluence. My day job is as the co-owner of KL&P, a marketing company in the Silicon Valley. Our largest single account is AT&T, and they had just purchased two telecommunications companies in Mexico. One was owned by Nextel and another by Carlos Slim. They were in the process of planning to rebrand over 2000 stores with the AT&T globe. Theresa Garland, one of their marketing directors and a dear client of ours for many years, approached my partner Jennifer Katz and me. We began devising a plan to raise awareness for AT&T's entry into the Mexico market by engaging Latinos in both countries with a social media campaign. On Facebook, a glass of filthy water appeared. As you shook your phone, the glass of water cleared up, a little. You were prompted to shake it again, and the dirty water cleared to reveal a message, in Spanish, to share this game with others and help bring safe drinking water to families. For each share, AT&T would donate $1 to H2OpenDoors in order to create purified water plants in Mexico.

This turned out to be one of the most successful social media campaigns that AT&T ever created. Within two weeks, we were presented with a check for $50,000, allowing us to build two water plants. The SunSprings proudly carry the AT&T Globe and the H2OpenDoors logo, and the people of Mexico got a good look at the soul of a company.

As I mentioned, we always return one year later. In between our second visits, we're in communications with the village or the local Rotary club or NGO partner to make sure the monthly maintenance procedures are being followed, and to answer any questions or concerns. When we return to install another system in the nearby region, we inspect the condition of the SunSpring and talk with the technicians. We quiz them on their retained knowledge and are never surprised to learn that they treat the SunSpring as their own pride and joy. This is the final payoff for me. It has trained my neural pathways to crave a continued hit of a high that can't be duplicated in a chemical way. So, I start the process all over again. I call Jack, Michelle, Brad, Alex, Mary Jo, Liz and the rest of the gang. "Hey kids, let's put on a show!"

IT HASN'T ALWAYS BEEN ROSY

The 2015 Rotary convention was held in Sao Paulo, Brazil. Jack Barker and I were on our way to the Sao Paulo International Airport returning to the USA after five days. We had been meeting with clusters of the 35,000 attendees from all over the world about H2OpenDoors, at my exhibit space in the House of Friendship. We felt tired and satisfied. We were in an Uber car, a black Toyota, on the freeway. I was in the passenger seat, and Jack was in the back seat. It was 8PM, dark, and we were on the freeway.

The traffic was stopped about 10 miles away from the airport. I was looking at my emails on my iPhone when I heard a rapping on the driver's window. I didn't look up right away, because I assumed it was someone selling flowers. It was a young man with crazed eyes in a green t-shirt pointing a gun at the driver and screaming in Portuguese. The driver gave him his cell phone and then his watch.

The gunman then pointed his Glock at me, screaming his Portuguese gibberish. The driver is telling me that he wants my phone. I didn't understand his words, but the terrified expression on his face and the eyes darting to my hand with the phone conveyed his plea with perfect clarity. I said something like "Fuck me" and handed the kid my phone.

The screaming continued, even more feverish, to give him my BRAND NEW APPLE WATCH. It was then that I sensed two additional people in the car. Not real people mind you. They were sitting on my shoulder. One, on my right shoulder, was Liam Neeson from the *Taken* movies. He whispered into my ear, "I possess certain unique skills that, when properly employed, will render you unconscious and immobile." The other person on my left shoulder, Mr. Catatonic, didn't say anything but had a frozen, wide-eyed expression. I began a series of calculations in what must have been 15 seconds, while I pretended to have trouble taking my watch off:

1. *Is there a magazine in the clip?*
2. *Where exactly is his finger at the trigger? On it or near it?*
3. *Can I reach his wrist by reaching over the driver?*
4. *Can I convince him to go around to the trunk and let me give him a duffle bag filled with a million dollars, so that I can be on equal footing with him in order to overpower him?*

It was on this last calculation that I hear the metallic slide cock sound of the gun. That prompted me to magically remove the watch and hand it to him. The traffic started to move, and he disappeared into the night.

My head was pounding and I felt a bit nauseous. I asked Jack to give me my backpack and used my iPad to launch the Find My Phone app to lock the watch and phone preventing access. Then I used Google Translate to converse with the driver. "Have you ever had a gun pointed at you?" I typed, the iPad speaking for me as a young Portuguese girl. The driver was still shaking a little but was focused on driving. He responded in Portuguese that he had not and that he wanted to pull the car over and cry. Firmly, I typed in all capitals, "WHATEVER YOU DO, DO NOT STOP THIS CAR UNTIL WE ARE AT THE AIRPORT!" The little girl voice translated this in a less convincing tone.

The driver called into his dispatcher about the incident on his personal phone. Handing it to me, the Uber manager spoke, in perfect English, "You need to go over to the nearest police station to report this." "*Are you kidding me?*" I responded. What would I report? A guy in a green shirt just robbed me. Are they likely to launch a dragnet in this city of 13 million? I told him that he should report it, but that I'm getting the hell out of Brazil NOW.

I haven't told this story to a lot of people. Not to my partners, who graciously give me the space to travel to dangerous places to do what I do, not to certain friends and relatives who would worry about me in the future or hassle me with judgments I don't care to hear. When you go to regions with rampant desperation, there are risks. My eyes are open to this, and now even more vigilant.

My PTSD lasted for a few months after returning to the States. When you first arrive home after an incident like that, you want to kiss the ground as you step off your plane. America, I love you. But I kept harkening back to Lawrence of Arabia, who had faced perpetual danger in his adventures. When he was home, he was killed on a bicycle by a distracted driver. Not sure if that is factual, but it is how I remember it. So, Jon of America, traveling to some of the most desperate regions on the planet, almost got killed after a Rotary convention. Irony.

SURROUNDED BY UNSUNG HEROES

Take a look around you. There are pretty outstanding people in our midst. The media surmises that we get more satisfaction out of watching people fail or be exposed as a hypocrite. I know I prefer to hear about people who innovate, provide service, create a disruptive solution to age-old problems. As much as I abhor watching CNN for longer than 30 minutes, you've got to hand it to them. The CNN Heroes series they do every year is some good, soulful stuff. Many of the CBS local stations take part in naming local Jefferson Award winners, in recognizing their efforts for positive social impact. Celebrating the unselfishness of our peers makes for good TV, and therefore, great ratings. I want to see more of this. We have enough award shows for celebrities, thank you very much.

Andy Frisch is in my Rotary club in Redwood City, California. He's the Executive Director of Kainos, an organization that cares for and employs adults with challenges like Down syndrome. Andy and his staff put on numerous events that feature the clients in red carpet-like roles. The hundreds of supporters of Kainos love to come to these events. The shadows are lifted on these folks, filled with love and dreams of their own.

My cousin in ChicagoLand, Melinda Deuster, is a great hero of mine as well. Her youngest son, Ross, recently died of a drug overdose. We don't know if it was accidental or purposeful, but we do know Ross was dealing with an uphill battle with mental illness. Mel is a wonderful advocate for families dealing with this. She has taught me not to judge. Some people we walk the Earth with are carrying a heavier load than we can ever imagine.

Dayani Centeno-Torres and her husband Ricardo Soto Diaz are a powerhouse couple in Puerto Rico. Few have the dedication to make fundamental changes on this island, so vulnerable to Mother Nature's wrath and Father America's indifference. He's an attorney and she is a communications expert. Together they put on seminars at dozens of communities, guiding them to create their own micro grids and purified water systems. They asked for H2OpenDoors' help with a SunSpring for the hardest-hit community of Punta Santiago. We've since installed six community water plants and continue to support the decentralization of infrastructure on this most vulnerable island.

In 2018, I lost my very best friend for over half of my life. Barry Levine was a bear of a man in size and spirit. It was not uncommon for Barry and Maddi to be at an airport and go up to a crew of young Army recruits on their way to battle handing out wads of cash. I would watch him interact with strangers during our vacations to Cambodia or Panama and dozens of other places. His kindness and humor was infectious and he brightened their day. Barry was a maven, as described by Malcolm Gladwell in *Tipping Point*. You want a restaurant or travel tip in one of hundreds of cities in the world, you would call "the Bubba." He is desperately missed.

Wendy Williams is the ultimate connector, also described by Gladwell, and has been a friend for over 40 years. As a Citizen Ambassador of the US State Department, Wendy and her husband Tommy open their home and hearts to visitors from all over the world. Each year, the State Department invites thousands of foreign guests to experience and learn what the real America is all about.

People like Wendy demonstrate and represent our heart and soul, fostering respect and understanding with context.

Peter Lagarius co-founded Rotaplast in 1992 as a project of the Rotary Club of San Francisco. A surgical program to Chile to treat children with severe cleft lip and palate anomaly has grown to hundreds of surgical missions in dozens of countries. Closing in on 20,000 patients, Rotaplast is now a separate nonprofit. They deserve our support. *See a need, provide an answer.* Peter is a role model for many of us in Rotary throughout the world.

Another Rotarian, Keith Axtell, tirelessly works to promote Rotary's programs for microfinance to the poorest of the poor. Christopher Major teaches strategy and tolerance to children with his innovative Novato Chess Club concept. Barry Jolette, recently retired as CEO of San Mateo Credit Union, grew that institution to be a solid financial center in the Silicon Valley. But it was his work in the communities and support for innovative start-up ideas for people all over the world we all celebrate the most. And so it goes. We are surrounded by people that devote their time to helping others. You might not see them on a CNN Heroes special, but they deserve a random act of kindness from all of us.

Ultimately, H2OpenDoors isn't really a water project at all. It's more about *Self-Reliance and Dignity.* We want to give a kick start to villages and schools who've been getting the short end of the stick for generations. By accident of birth, those caught in generational poverty appeared on the planet at a profound disadvantage. Those of us who blipped onto the scene, shot out of a womb and into a life of relative privilege, can do something with very little effort or funds. If we are strategic about it. We can raise human dignity at the same time. We can bring opportunity for our doppelgangers in very poor countries. What they do with it is important to me. We hope they become self-reliant citizens who can *pay it forward.*

TEN RANDOM SUGGESTIONS TO CHANGE THE WORLD

1. My number one wish is that all governments would officially declare that water, along with air and freedom, is a Human Right. Even Gandhi couldn't push that boulder up the hill. But I do have a recommendation. Use cost analysis for all things related to water. It shouldn't cost 1/3 to 1/2 of a person's daily income for water. Let's kick the bottled water industry in the shins with laws that forbid gouging. Set a limit for the price of water. Think I'm a socialist for suggesting this? All water is ultimately the property of all of us. It evaporates and forms clouds above us all. The clouds get too heavy and they rain down on us all, and then hopefully recharge our dams, lakes, rivers and aquifers. No one has an exclusive claim on water, just as no one can monopolize our air. We're using the same hydrogen/oxygen molecules we've had since the Big Bang. Dinosaurs drank it up, urinated it back into the soil, where it mixed in with underground streams. Who can lay claim to these molecules that have recirculated through our ecosystems for over four and a half billion years?

2. Don't allow the single-use bottle anymore. Bring back the water dispensers. Used to be that drinking water fountains were everywhere. Now, you only see the fancy ones in the best airports. They're wonderful, and you can fill up your reusable bottle, once you're past security, for free.

3. Speaking of reusable bottles, let's start a fashion trend. This might require the talents of the much-maligned Kardashian clan. Holsters and slings that hold reusable water bottles. Make them sexy and cool. Statement-makers, these accessories could also have some futuristic sensors operating communication, cooling, battery capacity, heart monitoring and threat analysis. The ultimate wearable device.

4. Make Sales a required class in High School. STEM should be STEMS. Science, Technology, Engineering, Math and Sales. Learning how to sell your idea, your point of view, your innovation–this is a skill badly needed for those in STEM, and in any occupation on the planet. The art of persuasion, to be a convincer–our kids suck at it. If we don't give them the real-world tactics and strategies to sell themselves, they will face continued obstacles. In addition, those who actually want to sell to make their living have the potential to make a lot of money with a maximum amount of control over their time. Think, for a moment, of the wealthiest people you know–in your family, on your block. I'll wager that at least 1/3 of them are in sales. The other 2/3 are excellent at selling their vision, their direction. Confidence is learned, not inherited.

5. Speaking of selling, let's teach our young college students that the endpoint of your ridiculously expensive university experience doesn't have to mean a job at Google or Apple or Facebook.

All wonderful companies to join, no doubt. But there is a heap of need in the badly-named nonprofit sector. Organizations doing the hard work to make the world a better place for the poorest of the poor need you. Use your newly acquired selling skills to disrupt the broken and tired methods of fundraising. Come up with new ways to excite and inspire the rest of us to support a project or a cause.

6. Speaking of projects and causes—no matter how passionate you are to solve a problem, you don't need to start your own 501(c)(3) nonprofit. You can collaborate with others, join a service organization like Rotary or Lions, and work on any issue you want. You would be surprised how much support you'll get. These are "power packs of passion" you can plug into.

7. Speaking of plugs, this is where I shamelessly pitch H2OpenDoors to those of you that have read this far. Thank you. If you are so moved, go to *www.H2OpenDoors.org*. You can certainly donate. You can also participate on one of our many voluntourism expeditions. We'd love to have you join us. As country rocker Darius Rucker asks, "*When was the last time you did something for the first time?*" Mostly, we need you to spread the word about what we're doing. The more traction we can get, the more good we can do. And we want to do it with you!

8. Speaking of speaking, may I suggest joining Toastmasters? Just as Rotary is the gold standard for service organizations, Toastmasters International is the best place to hone your personal and professional communication skills. You'll meet young professionals and established business people of all races, from all sorts of places. The one-hour weekly meetings, often with breakfast, are fast paced, mostly everyone taking on a role. You

can be a speaker, an evaluator, a grammarian and more. Bonus: it's cheap! You'll network with new friends who want you to excel and learn something about your potential every single time.

9. The line between opinion and the news is getting too blurry. Here's an idea for members of the national media corps: Let's find an independent organization that all sides can agree upon to be the official fact checker. Devote five minutes to every broadcast that is over one-half hour to self-examination. Reviews of the previous day's Top Three reports with an objective True/False analysis would go a long way towards balance. By the way, because the airwaves are public property, put an "Opinion" caption under the talking head when one of the reporters or anchors launches into a diatribe. Personally, I want to reach my own conclusions about the whys and hows of the news. *Just tell me what happened today* and keep the snark and hidden agendas out of it, please. Reporters seem to view their jobs as prosecutors, representing the left or the right. While I appreciate the comfort of living in one's own echo chamber to reinforce what you already believe, journalism is supposed to inform and enlighten.

10. If you reached this last suggestion by the old-fashioned method of reading a book from front to back, thank you from the bottom of my heart. If you got here, as I often do, by scanning, flipping through and attempting to reach the Executive Summary without all the fluff, then thank you, but not as much. I can identify with the feeling of being overwhelmed by messages every day. We are naturally jealous of our time. You spent some of it reading or listening to this, my first book. You've indulged me, perhaps gotten a few insights about your path, and hopefully

enjoyed a giggle or two. Let's start a dialogue, shall we? I look forward to meeting you.

Finally, I would like to point out that inspiration doesn't come as a bolt of lightning to me. I might wake up, startled, with a thought that I can't get out of my head. In my marketing work, that's how it usually happens. An idea to help a client breakthrough the clutter, or a cool logo design idea. For me, inspiration is something more slow burning. Sometimes more like a fever. Other times like a tiny rock in my sock I'm forced to pay attention to. It took me four full years to do something about my promise to Jaye, starting the H2OpenDoors project. And then another four years to realize that H2OpenDoors really isn't about water at all. It's about Self-Reliance and Dignity. The lack of both was causing my sister's tears as we witnessed the Haitians descend from the jungled mountains, gleaning the trash for leftovers of our feast that day on Labadie. No family should be relegated to a life of squalor, and she showed me that when you are witness to horror, you can't look away with indifference. You must be accountable to another person and make a promise. Only through promise, can you follow up and pay forward any good fortune you have.

Protest is not a promise. It is catharsis. It is free speech. It is necessary. But it's not a promise of accountability. It doesn't lay out what your personal responsibility is. What promise can you make to someone, when you know they will soon be gone, that will cause you to bestow honor on their memory? Have that conversation with them right now. It's important.

This has been my journey of the past six years. It has been a learning experience. The mistakes I've made have been lessons I hope will save you some grief as you take off on your path. The few things I've done right include surrounding myself with magnificent people who, for reasons of their own, keep coming back to play. I am eternally grateful. Peace out.

Notes:

1. On research by Frantisek Kozisek: *http://www.who.int/water_sanitation_health/dwq/nutrientschap12.pdf*

2. On research about the Life Straw: *https://ssir.org/articles/entry/thirty_million_dollars_a_little_bit_of_carbon_and_a_lot_of_hot_air*

AUTHOR BIOGRAPHY

Jon Kaufman started the H2OpenDoors project within Rotary in 2012 after several years of interest and philanthropy in the area of safe drinking water for villages, schools and hospitals in the developing world.

Since 1989, Jon has been co-owner of a Silicon Valley marketing company, Kaufman, Levine & Partners. Working with large corporations, he has developed innovative approaches to employee engagement for safety and productivity improvement. KL&P's core business is providing promotional marketing strategy and support.

With a growing passion to apply technology to some of the most grinding challenges in the developing world, Jon has been focused on water, education and community self-reliance. He has assembled a team of 80 experienced and soulful experts in their fields in over nine countries.

Jon lives with his girlfriend, Michelle Nirenstein, in San Carlos, California. Their three children are grown and on their own, so they have started over with three dogs.

To stay on top of the news and expeditions with H2OpenDoors, check out *www.H2OpenDoors.org* and Facebook.com/H2OpenDoors. You can also reach Jon at *jon@H2OpenDoors.org*. Your support needs to be earned. All proceeds from the sale of *Long Walk on a Dry Road* will go to the operating fund of the H2OpenDoors project.